The Complete Renal Diet Cookbook for Beginners

100 Easy and Low-salt Recipes with 4-week Meal Plan to Manage Kidney Disease and Avoid Dialysis

Dennis P. Cook

CONTENT

Introduction

Consisted of perfectly integrated systems, the human body is a real marvel. There's good news and bad news about this, though. The good news is that what you do with one of these systems can help other systems get better when they are diseased.

The bad news?

Well, what you do with one of these systems can affect other systems and spread disease to them.

There's no such thing as a 100% independent, stand-alone body part in the human body. Everything is connected. Everything works together to help us move, talk, cry, and love. Everything is brought together to create the top of the food chain: **Homo Sapiens**.

There's a good reason the "food chain" was mentioned here, and it doesn't have anything to do with whether or not you are a vegan, a vegetarian, or an omnivore. The reason food was brought into discussion here is because food plays a vital role in health.

What you eat influences your entire body. Food fuels everything from how you look and how your skin and hair shine bright in the sunlight to how you think, how you sleep, and how every single organ in your body functions in its correct parameters.

That is precisely why a healthy diet is essential to a good life.

In this book, we will discuss a very specific type of diet: the renal diet. Targeting people who suffer from chronic kidney disease, the renal diet was designed to help them live better, happier, and healthier lives.

No, chronic disease cannot be cured. But with the right medical and societal support and with the right diet, patients suffering from chronic kidney diseases can get better and live happy, normal lives.

Are you ready to step into a life where you can control the outcome of your chronic kidney disease?

If so, turn the page and let's dive right into the nitty-gritty of everything renal diet-related.

Chapter 1: Kidney Disease Basics to Remember

The human body is a perfectly imperfect mechanism. Every single cell in your body is part of a larger story. Every tissue, every organ, and every system has a very clearly defined purpose. Along with their specific function, different systems are very tightly connected to each other.

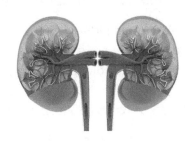

How you breathe, for example, affects every other part of your body. Your blood circulation can also have a powerful effect on every organ in your body. And what you eat and drink will definitely affect everything as well.

Knowing how your kidneys work and what they actually "do" in your body is essential for your understanding of the renal diet. In this chapter, we will discuss the role of the kidney system in the human body, some of the most common chronic kidney diseases, their symptoms, the stages of disease, the treatments, as well as how patients can receive support.

Let's dive deeper into these topics!

NATIONAL KIDNEY FOUNDATION.

A chronic kidney disease is a disease that has shown repetitive, consistent influences over the health of a patient. Causes for kidney diseases can include diabetes, high blood pressure, and congenital conditions. The most common causes for chronic kidney disease will be discussed in the next section, along with the most notable risk factors you should be aware of.

As a general rule, there is no actual cure for any kind of chronic disease **(the very definition of a "chronic" disease means that it's a lifelong condition).** However, with modern treatment and support, most chronic kidney diseases (and chronic diseases as a general rule) can be successfully managed and patients can live long, happy, and normal lives.

Adjusting diet is an important part of the treatment plan for chronic diseases.

How Kidneys Work and Their Role in the Human Body

The main role of the kidney is to filter the blood in your body. Basically, kidneys filter all the blood that goes through your body, and they do this several times every day. Their goal is to ensure the fluid balance and electrolyte levels in the blood.

When blood comes into a kidney, the waste gets removed, and the elements in it are adjusted (such as salt, water, and minerals, for example). Once filtered, the blood goes back into the body. Everything that's waste becomes urine, which is collected in the pelvis and then gets drained down through the ureter to the bladder.

Kidneys are not only part of a system (as explained in the previous paragraph). They are also micro-systems on their own that consist of approximately one million nephrons (which are basically very small filters).

As you can imagine, kidneys are extremely important in the human body. They filter the blood and are a central element to removing waste products, such as drugs, from the body. Furthermore, kidneys also release hormones that regulate blood pressure, control the production of red blood cells, and release a form of vitamin D that helps your bones stay strong and healthy.

The biggest issues that can develop in the kidney are a byproduct of blood stopping from its flow through this filtering system. In these cases, part or even the entirety of the kidney could die. That is the very worst case scenario, though, and most definitely not the only way kidneys could get sick. We will discuss more about this in the following section of this chapter.

Causes and Risk Factors

There are many causes and risk factors that are very tightly connected to kidney disease. Below, we will discuss some of the most common ones — but keep in mind that there might be other causes for chronic kidney disease too.

Diabetes

Diabetes is one of the leading causes for kidney disease. It may seem the two are not necessarily connected, but as mentioned before, pretty much everything in the human body is connected at one level or another.

Diabetes is a disease associated with an unhealthily low level of insulin (and, in some cases, improper use of normal amounts of insulin). This leads to high blood sugar levels, which can be an issue for many parts of your body — kidneys included.

More specifically, diabetes can damage the blood vessel clusters that filter the blood in the kidneys. When this happens, kidney damage and high blood pressure can develop.

High Blood Pressure

Along with diabetes, high blood pressure is also very commonly associated with kidney problems. In very simple terms, high blood pressure (also known as hypertension) develops when the force of blood against artery walls increases. When high blood pressure is not controlled, a series of complications can develop — including heart attacks, strokes, and kidney disease.

Hypertension can cause the arteries around the kidneys to change their structure (they can narrow, harden, or weaken). In consequence, the kidney will not receive enough blood through these arteries — and, in time, kidney damage can develop.

It is also worth mentioning that the relationship between kidneys and high blood pressure can also 'move' in an opposite direction. For instance, if a patient's adrenal glands (located near the kidney) do not work properly, he/she might develop high blood pressure.

Other Kidney Disease Issues

In addition to diabetes and high blood pressure, there is a series of kidney disease issues you might want to be aware of, including (but not limited to) the following (National Kidney Foundation, n.d.):

1. **Glomerulonephritis.** This is a disease that damages the glomeruli, which are the filtering units in the kidney. This health issue can develop suddenly (such as after a strep throat) and the patient can get well again. However, the issue can also develop slowly over the years, which can lead to progressive loss of kidney function.

2. **Polycystic kidney disease.** This is one of the most common inherited kidney problems. As its name suggests, this disease is characterized by the presence of kidney cysts. In time, they can enlarge and lead to severe kidney damage. In the worst case scenarios, kidney failure can happen as well.

3. **Kidney stones.** These are extremely common — and passing them can cause very high levels of pain in your back and your side. When kidney stones are too large to be passed naturally, treatments can be applied to break the stones into smaller pieces that can be eliminated by the human body. Kidney stones can form as a result of an inherited disorder (such as when too much calcium is absorbed from foods, for example). Diet and medication can prevent the recurrent forming of kidney stones.

4. **Urinary tract infection.** These are also very common, and they occur when germs reach the urinary tract. Symptoms include pain and burning during urination, as well as the need to urinate more frequently. These infections are most likely to affect the bladder, but in the worst case scenarios they spread to the kidneys causing fever and back pain.

5. **Congenital diseases.** These issues develop most frequently during pregnancy when the baby is developing in its mother's womb. For example, some babies are born with issues that make the valve-like mechanism between the bladder and ureter work improperly. This can cause the baby to urinate back up into the kidneys, which can lead to infections and kidney damage.

6. **Drug and toxin-related kidney issues.** Sometimes, using over the counter pain medication for extended periods of time can harm the kidneys. Using other medications, pesticides, as well as street drugs (such as heroin) can also lead to kidney damage.

Symptoms

Symptoms for chronic kidney disease might differ from one patient to another depending on their specific situation, as well as the leading cause and risk factors that generated the kidney disease in the first place.

Some of the most commonly encountered chronic kidney disease symptoms include the following (NHS, 2019):

- Swollen ankles, feet, or hands (a sign of water retention)
- Tiredness and fatigue
- Blood in urine
- Weight loss and poor appetite
- Shortness of breath
- Increased urination frequency
- Sleep difficulties
- Itchy skin
- Headaches
- Erectile dysfunctions (in men)
- Feeling sick
- Muscle cramps

Stages of Chronic Kidney Disease (CKD)

To help physicians and specialist doctors determine how advanced a chronic kidney disease is, the patient will be tested for their Glomerular Filtration Rate (also known as GFR) (Davita, n.d.-a). According to the results, the patient's diagnosis will fall in one of the five stages of CKD development:

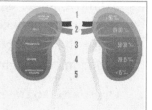

- Stage 1: **normal or high GFR (GFR > 90 mL/ min)**
- Stage 2: **mild CKD (GFR = 60-89 mL/min)**
- Stage 3A: **moderate CKD (GFR = 45-59 mL/min)**
- Stage 3B: **moderate CKD (GFR = 30-44 mL/min)**
- Stage 4: **severe CKD (GFR = 15-29 mL/min)**
- Stage 5: **end stage CKD (GFR < 16 mL/ min)**

Knowing what stage a patient's chronic disease is at is important because it will help doctors apply the right type of treatment. Each of these stages has its specificities, and although we do not aim to get too in-depth with this topic here, there are some basics you might want to know, as follows:

Stage 1 and 2

In addition to measuring the GFR levels, there are other telltale signs of chronic kidney disease at this stage (Davita, n.d.-b):

- Higher levels of creatinine or urea in blood

- Blood in the urine

- Protein in the urine

- MRI, CT scan, ultrasound, or contrast X-ray shows evidence of kidney damage

- Having a family history of polycystic kidney disease

Stage 3 (A and B)

Likewise, Stage 3 kidney disease can show other symptoms and signs when the diagnosis process is applied (Davita, n.d.-c):

- Fatigue

- Swelling of extremities

- Fluid retention

- Shortness of breath

- Changes in the urine (foamy, dark orange, brow, or tea-colored, or even red when it contains blood)

- Urination frequency changes (urinating more or less than normal)

- Kidney pain (resented in the back area)

- Sleep issues related to muscle cramps or restless legs

Stage 4

In addition to the symptoms mentioned at Stage 3, Stage 4 patients can develop additional signs and symptoms showing the degree of their chronic kidney disease (Davita, n.d.-d):

- Feeling a metallic taste in the mouth

- Urea buildup in the blood, which leads to bad breath

- Loss of appetite

- Concentration difficulties (even when it comes to everyday tasks)

- Nervous system issues (such as numbness or tingling in the extremities)

Stage 5

In addition to all the aforementioned symptoms. Stage 5 patients in chronic kidney disease may also report (Davita, n.d.-e):

- Itching sensations

- Changes in skin color

- Increased skin pigmentation

Treatments

The treatment applied to patients suffering from chronic kidney disease differs, according to the root cause of their issues, as well as the degree of evolution in the disease.

In general, patients in Stage 1, 2, and 3 (A and B) will be recommended the following solutions:

- A healthy diet focusing on whole grains, fresh fruits and veggies, low saturated fats, and low on sodium. We will discuss more about this in Chapter 2 of this book

- Maintaining the blood pressure at healthy levels (which differs depending on whether or not the patient has diabetes or proteinuria)

- Maintaining blood sugar and keeping diabetes under control

- Having regular checkups with the doctor

- Running GFR tests

- Take medicine prescribed by the doctor

- Exercising with regularity

- Stop smoking

For patients in Stage 4 and 5, additional treatments will be applied in most cases. These treatments include:

- Hemodialysis (removing small portions of the patient's blood, to clean out the toxins kidneys can no longer filter, and then returning the blood to the patient's body)

- Peritoneal dialysis (also known as "PD", a needle-free procedure similar in concept with hemodialysis, but which does not require a care treatment)

- Kidney transplant (which might not be available for Stage 5 patients)

In all cases, though, diet plays a crucial role in managing chronic kidney condition. While medication and other more or less intrusive treatments are available, none will actually have the desired effect if the patient's diet doesn't shift for better food choices.

Getting Support

Patients diagnosed with chronic kidney disease will need support, so it is of the utmost importance that you find the best solutions for you. Some options for getting support when you have CKD include the following:

- Healthcare providers

- Physicians

- Social workers

- Nurses

- Dietitians

- Family and friends

You don't have to be alone in this (and, in fact, you should not be alone). Ask for help to feel supported in your journey of slowing down kidney disease and regaining the power of your life.

Chapter 2: Slowing Down Kidney Diseases with the Renal Diet

As mentioned before, your diet plays a crucial role in slowing down kidney disease and learning how to manage it throughout your life.

Although changing your lifestyle and diet is not easy (sometimes, the changes can be quite extreme), this is a necessary step your body needs to be able to withstand chronic kidney disease.

The good news is that these days, you have all the information you need to put together a dietary plan that really works for you — and doesn't deprive you of the pleasure of eating (and living your life as beautifully as you want it).

In this chapter, we will expand more on the renal diet: what it is, what its main purpose is, what are the main guidelines to keep in mind, as well as how to implement this diet into your life in a smooth, hassle-free way.

What is The Renal Diet ?

The renal diet is crucial in the management of chronic kidney disease. It might mean you have to make serious changes in how you eat, but it also means that it will give you a fuller life in which pain and health issues do not prevent you from actually enjoying the beautiful moments.

The renal diet is a dietary approach that focuses on making your kidneys' job as easy as possible, so that they do not get strained in the filtering process they run on a daily basis.

As you will see further on in this chapter, the renal diet comes with a series of guidelines. These "rules" are not really flexible, and as someone suffering from chronic disease, you should definitely take the time to understand how all this works. It might not be easy at first, but it will soon become part of your daily routine.

The main purpose of the renal diet is to balance out the levels of minerals, electrolytes, and fluids in the body. In the case of patients who are on dialysis, special attention has to be put into making sure they lower the amount of waste in their bodies as much as possible (so that their kidneys can function in normal parameters).

Guidelines for the Renal Diet

The rules of the renal diet are built around the idea that you need to have a low intake of certain minerals, electrolytes, and fluids — so that your kidneys' job is as easy as possible.

The main guidelines for the renal diet are the following:

Limit Sodium Intake

Sodium intake should be limited at 2,000 milligrams per day. This means that you will have to pay quite a lot of attention to making sure what you eat is as low-sodium as possible because it is extremely easy to go over this limit.

For instance, the vast majority of highly processed foods are also very high in sodium — so they should be avoided altogether. The more you cook with fresh, whole ingredients, the more likely it is that you will stay away from high-sodium meals.

It is quite important to check the sodium levels of everything you put in your foods. You can find these on the labels (usually measured in milligrams of sodium per a given quantity of the product, which also means you might have to invest in kitchen scales).

Furthermore, keep in mind that you can find a lot of products in their low-sodium versions. In general, you want to avoid anything that's overprocessed — but if you absolutely have to have it, use the low-sodium version at all times.

As a general rule of thumb, the following foods are considered to be high in sodium:

- Processed meats (such as through smoking, curing, salting, or canning)

- Frozen breaded meats

- Canned foods (such as canned spam, ravioli, or chilli)

- Salted nuts

- Canned beans (if they have added salt; this information should be available on the label)

Limit Potassium Intake

Just like sodium, potassium intake should be carefully measured as well. People with CKD should not intake more than 2,000 milligrams of potassium every day.

In addition to checking the potassium on all the ingredients you put in your foods (and making sure you adequately measure each of them as well), you might also have to consider the following solutions to ensure you are getting just enough potassium from your diet:

- Avoiding salt substitutes (as many of them have a low level of sodium, but a high level of potassium)

- Avoiding herbal supplements, particularly if they were not prescribed to you by a medical body

- Taking water pills or potassium binders, but only if they are prescribed to you by a doctor

In general, the following foods are considered to be high in potassium. While you may not have to eliminate them completely from your diet, you should probably be quite careful of how much of these foods you eat:

- Bananas
- Grapefruit
- Apricot
- Oranges
- Dried fruit
- Cooked spinach

- Cooked broccoli
- Sweet potatoes and potatoes
- Mushrooms
- Peas
- Cucumbers

Limit Phosphorus Intake

Too much phosphorus can also be harmful, especially for people suffering from chronic kidney disease. In general, patients with CKD should make sure to not exceed 800 to 1,000 milligrams of phosphorus intake per day.

This means that you should avoid the following foods and drinks as much as possible:

- Any fast food (including packaged, convenience, and gas station foods)
- Processed cheeses (such as cheese spreads)
- Meats that have added flavor to them (regardless of whether they are fresh or frozen)
- Cola and pepper-type drinks
- Flavored waters
- Bottled teas
- Energy and sports drinks
- Powdered drink mixes
- Beer
- Wine

Lean Protein Sources

Getting your proteins from lean sources is also quite important when it comes to managing chronic kidney disease correctly. Furthermore, it is also important to measure the amount of protein you take from your food and to not exceed your daily necessary protein (which should be calculated by a healthcare provider).

Some of the best protein sources to consider include the following:

- **Lean burgers.** You don't have to give up on burgers altogether. As long as they are made from lean turkey or chicken, you can have them

- **Chicken.** One of the easiest to cook and versatile meats out there, chicken is a good choice in a wide variety of diets (including the renal diet)

- **Cottage cheese.** Due to the low sodium level and high level of proteins, cottage cheese is also a good choice for the renal diet

- **Deviled eggs.** As long as you do not add too much salt to your deviled eggs, they can be a good choice for your diet

- **Egg omelette.** There are many ways to make an omelette, but most times, it will be a healthy choice for people on a renal diet. The one thing to avoid is adding processed meat or high sodium cheese to your omelette

- **Egg whites.** One of the best ways to limit the amount of cholesterol in your omelette is by including more egg whites (which are also a good source of lean proteins)

- **Fish.** Not only is fish a great source of protein, but, as you will see in the following section, a lot of types of fish are also a good source of healthy fats

- **Greek yogurt.** Great for breakfast and for a quick snack, greek yogurt is another good source of protein. However, you should probably settle on the low-fat version, as this will have less of an impact on your heart health. Also, keep in mind that greek yogurt functions best when it's eaten as a meat replacement (meaning that, due to the high amount of protein in it, you might want to balance out greek yogurt and meats in your diet)

- **Meat substitutes.** Veggie burgers and veggie sausages can be a good source of lean protein, but it is also important to watch their sodium and potassium quantities

- **Nutrition drinks.** There is a series of nutrition drinks created especially for people on a renal diet, which can work out very well as protein sources. It is important to check with your dietitian, though, to make sure you balance things out correctly

- **Pork chops.** It might sound unbelievable to find pork on a list of healthy foods, but pork chops can be a good choice of high-quality protein, thiamine, and iron

- **Protein bars and protein powder/ liquid supplements.** Just like with nutrition drinks, you should check with your doctor or dietitian before you start taking any kind of protein-based supplement. It might be a good choice for you, but balance is key here

- **Tofu cheese.** A great vegan replacement for cheese, tofu is also great in terms of protein intake. However, make sure to check its sodium and potassium content!

Heart Healthy Fats

Since heart health and kidney health are intrinsically connected, it is also quite important to eat as many healthy fats as you can (as well as limit the intake of saturated fats and cholesterol in general).

Heart healthy fats are usually found in the following foods:

- Seeds (sunflower, pumpkin, or sesame, but it is important to avoid the salty ones, as they have a high level of sodium)

- Flaxseed

- Walnuts (likewise, without salt)

- Fatty fish (such as tuna, salmon, trout, sardines, or herring, for example)

- Soybean and sunflower oil

- Soymilk

- Tofu cheese

- Avocado

- Olives (low-sodium versions)

- Peanut butter

At the same time, the following foods should be avoided, as they are high in unhealthy, trans, and saturated fats:

- Any kind of commercial pastry, cookies, muffins, pizza, or cake dough

- Snack foods like crackers, microwave popcorn, or chips

- Stick margarine

- Fried foods (they should all be avoided)

- Foods containing hydrogenated and partially hydrogenated oil (even when it claims to be trans fat-free)

- Any kind of red meat (including beef, lamb, and pork)

- Chicken skin

- Whole-fat dairy products (including cheese, cream, and milk)

- Butter and lard

- Ice cream

- Coconut oil

- Palm oil

High Fiber Carbs

Contrary to the popular belief these days, carbs are not our enemies. On the contrary, the human body needs carbs — but it is also essential that your carb intake comes from high-fiber sources. This is important because it will promote digestive system health, as well as heart health (because it helps with the absorption of fats in the intestines).

Some of the best sources of high fiber carbs include the following:

Unpeeled apples	Raw cabbage	Pears
Apricots	Lettuce	Corn
Asparagus	Carrots	Summer squash
Beets	Celery	Raw pineapple
Berries	Onions	
Green beans	Cherries	

It is very important to note that some foods may be high in quality fiber while also being high in potassium. As mentioned in the section dedicated to potassium intake, you can't and should not eliminate all potassium-rich foods from your diet. However, you should be careful how much of these foods you get into your day. Measuring them with precision is the safest way to make sure you are not getting too much, or too little, potassium.

Calorie Counting and Portion Control

One of the main reasons people fail at diets (renal or not) is because, although they do eat healthy foods, they also eat them in unhealthy amounts. It's extremely common to misinterpret how much of a certain food you should eat and how large a serving size should be.

Cereal is notorious for this kind of mistake. While most people fill up their bowl with cereal, the normal serving size is, in most cases, a lot smaller than that.

It goes the same with pretty much every other type of food. Making excess amounts is quite common, and that is precisely why it is important to know what a regular serving size looks like for every type of food. For instance, you shouldn't eat more white meat than the size of your palm (fingers included) and you shouldn't eat more red meat than the size of your palm (fingers not included).

Last, but definitely not least, it is also very important to measure your calorie intake. Everything can lead to weight gain and health problems if it's not consumed in the right quantities and calorie counting can help you prevent that.

Calorie Counter

One of the easiest ways to count your calories is to install an app on your phone. There are many of them that are completely free and will help you keep track of your daily calorie intake.

As for how much your calorie intake should be, a medical body or dietitian can help you calculate that according to your gender, age, Body Mass Index, and level of activity. Together with your calorie intake, they will also calculate how much of each macronutrient and mineral you should take from your food.

Renal Supplements

In some cases, the doctor may also prescribe renal supplements. Although it is not necessarily the norm to take these, renal supplements can help you stay on track from a dietary point of view and make sure your body is getting just enough of every type of nutrient.

Fluid Intake

In most cases, fluid intake does not have to be controlled. However, for patients in Stage 5, the doctor may make recommendations as to how much fluid the patients should have on a daily basis. This is extremely important because it can affect the success rate of the treatments applied at this stage of chronic kidney disease development.

Implementing the Renal Diet on Special Occasions

Adhering to a stricter diet can feel like you are putting your entire social life on halt. We tend to place eating meals with others quite high on the scale of importance. Because of this, when someone withdraws from unhealthy eating behaviors, it might feel that they are also withdrawing themselves from social gatherings.

However, that does not have to be the case. Chronic kidney disease can be managed with a diet that doesn't necessarily prevent you from doing the things you love. It will take a little bit of dedicated attention at first, but over time healthier choices will just become your second nature.

Here are some examples on how to implement the renal diet on special occasions:

Dining Out

The best way to make sure you make good food choices when you are dining out is to plan ahead. If you know the restaurant and their menu, you will have more time to figure out which options they offer are better for you from a health perspective.

Furthermore, planning ahead also allows you to cut back on high sodium and high potassium foods throughout the day, before you dine out.

Lastly, remember to have your medication with you if you have been prescribed potassium binders or other pills.

Traveling

Traveling is one of the biggest pleasures in life and one of the most rewarding experiences. It can also feel like a massive temptation from a dietary point of view, especially since enjoying local foods can be, for many, one of travel's most important attractions.

With a little bit of planning, you can still travel while on the renal diet — and yes, you can still enjoy the beauties of doing this.

Some general ground rules for CKD patients traveling include the following:

- Bring a cooler that has healthy snacks in it with you to help you avoid fast food

- Keep the general renal diet guidelines in mind and stay away from things such as processed meats or fried foods

- Get low-sodium crackers and unsalted pretzels instead of potato chips

- If your doctor has prescribed you a fluid reduction, remember that salty foods can make you drink more water

- If you are attending a buffet, always lean towards the healthier area and eat things like veggies, fruit, and salads

- If you go on a cruise, let them know of your dietary needs, as they will be able to provide the correct options for your diet

- Avoid hot dogs, breaded fish, poultry, and fried foods by simply choosing healthier versions that are non-fried, not breaded, and leaner

- Likewise, replace french fries with a dinner roll or an English muffin

- If you only have high sodium options available, make sure to balance out your total daily intake by eating very low sodium options throughout the day

- Buy a phrase book to help you understand the ingredients in each food you eat

As tempting as "being away on travel" might be, it is also important for you to know there are plenty of dietary dangers waiting for you at home.

A normal night of movies and snacks can turn into a sodium and potassium feast without you even knowing.

Replacing chips with veggie sticks is a good way to have something clean and healthy to munch on. Likewise, salt-free popcorn can be a decent choice as well.

As for making dinner at home, you have literally hundreds, maybe even thousands of options that don't take much time to make, don't break the bank, and still allow you to stick to the renal diet.

FAQs about the Renal Diet

Understanding the renal diet is key to embracing it correctly. Therefore, we have put together a list of some of the most frequently asked questions in relation to this diet — as well as the answers that will help you figure this whole thing out.

1. What do the kidneys do?

As mentioned at the beginning of this book, the main role of the kidneys is to filter all the residue in the blood and make sure the waste is eliminated through urine.

2. What is a chronic kidney disease?

A chronic kidney disease is a disease that affects the good functioning of the kidneys. Usually, CKDs have a rather slow onset and they develop slowly over time — so they might not show symptoms right from the very beginning.

3. Is there any cure for CKD?

No. A "chronic" disease is, by definition, a disease that cannot be actually cured. CKD can, however, be managed very well.

4. What treatments are available for CKD?

There are many treatments and lifestyle solutions available for patients suffering from chronic kidney disease. They include dietary choices, exercising, weight loss, and stopping smoking, as well as medical treatments like drugs and dialysis.

5. Why is diet important in CKD management?

Diet is very important in managing CKD because it will allow you to control what goes into your kidneys. This will make their job much easier by reducing the strain you put on them.

6. Is dialysis always a treatment for CKD?

No, only patients in Stage 4 and Stage 5 CKD usually reach dialysis.

7. Is dialysis performed at home or in a center?

There are multiple types of dialysis available. Some are done in centers, others can be done at home with the help of a care partner, and others can be done at home without the presence of a care partner.

8. Does CKD irremediably lead to dialysis?

No, CKD does not always lead to dialysis. Diagnosed early and with proper care and attention, this condition can be successfully managed and kidney disease can be slowed down.

9. Is there any way to avoid keeping a diet?

No, not really. It is important for you to change your diet because otherwise, your issues will progress. Even in the case of a kidney transplant, you will still want to make sure you stick to a healthy renal diet to avoid issues from developing again.

10. Will I lose weight on the renal diet?

Chances are that, yes, you will lose weight on the renal diet. Although not necessarily the main goal, weight loss is likely to occur because the renal diet promotes healthy eating habits focused on balanced choices. Plus, weight loss is in itself a good way to help with CKD management as well, so it's a win-win on all fronts.

Taking on the renal diet does not have to mean you are consistently saddened by the loss of good food in your life. There are SO MANY delicious meals you can make that are just plain and simply good for you from every point of view! It might take a bit of practice until you nail everything correctly, but it will definitely become part of your habits.

And your entire body will thank you for your choices!

CHAPTER 3

BREAKFAST AND BRUNCH

Jelly and Peanut Butter Granola

Prep time: 15 minutes | Cook time: 30 minutes | Serves 6

- 2 cups rolled oats
- ¼ cup peanut butter
- 3 tablespoons maple syrup
- 1 tablespoon water
- ½ teaspoon ground cinnamon
- Pinch salt
- ¼ cup jelly, any flavor

1. Preheat the oven to 325ºF (163ºC). Line a rimmed baking sheet with parchment paper and set aside.
2. Pour the oats into a mixing bowl and set aside.
3. In a small saucepan, combine the peanut butter, maple syrup, water, cinnamon, and salt. Heat over low heat until the peanut butter is melted.
4. Pour the peanut butter mixture over the oats and toss to coat. Spread onto the baking sheet.
5. In a small bowl in the microwave or in a small pan on low heat, heat the jelly until it's thin, about 1 minute. Drizzle over the oat mixture on the baking sheet.
6. Bake for 20 to 30 minutes, stirring once during baking, until the granola is golden brown.
7. Cool completely and store in an airtight container at room temperature for up to a week.

Per Serving (¹/₃ cup)

calories: 231 | fat: 7.1g | carbs: 36.1g | phosphorus: 151mg | potassium: 191mg
sodium: 80mg | protein: 6.1g

Almond and Rice Cereal

Prep time: 5 minutes | Cook time: 7 hours | Serves 6

- 3 cups unsweetened almond milk
- 2 cups water
- 1½ cups wild rice, rinsed
- 1 cup brown rice
- ¼ cup maple syrup
- ⅛ teaspoon salt
- ²/₃ cup slivered almonds, toasted

1. In a slow cooker, combine the almond milk, water, wild rice, brown rice, maple syrup, and salt. Stir.
2. Cover and cook on low for 7 to 8 hours.
3. Top with the almonds and serve.

Per Serving

calories: 380 | fat: 8.9g | carbs: 66.2g | phosphorus: 340mg | potassium: 444mg
sodium: 141mg | protein: 10.9g

Turmeric and Squash Omelet

Prep time: 10 minutes | Cook time: 10 minutes | Serves 4

- 2 tablespoons extra-virgin olive oil
- ½ teaspoon ground turmeric
- 1 yellow bell pepper, chopped
- 1 small yellow summer squash, chopped
- 8 large eggs
- 1 tablespoon water
- Salt and freshly ground black pepper, to taste
- ½ cup shredded Colby cheese

1. In a medium nonstick skillet, heat the olive oil over medium heat. Add the turmeric and stir for 30 seconds, until fragrant.
2. Add the bell pepper and squash and cook for 3 to 5 minutes, or until tender, stirring occasionally. Transfer the vegetables to a plate and set aside; do not drain or wipe out the skillet.
3. Meanwhile, in a small bowl, beat the eggs with the water, salt, and pepper until frothy and combined. Add the egg mixture to the skillet.
4. Cook for 5 to 7 minutes, running a spatula around the edges of the omelet to let the uncooked portion flow under the cooked eggs, and shaking the pan occasionally, until the eggs are just set.
5. Top half of the omelet with the vegetable mixture and sprinkle with the cheese. With a spatula, fold the omelet in half and serve.

Per Serving

calories: 290 | fat: 21.8g | carbs: 5.1g | phosphorus: 266mg | potassium: 341mg
sodium: 212mg | protein: 17.2g

Raspberry and Watermelon Smoothie

Prep time: 10 minutes | Cook time: 0 minutes | Serves 2

- ½ cup boiled, cooled, and shredded red cabbage
- 1 cup diced watermelon
- ½ cup fresh raspberries
- 1 cup ice

1. Put the cabbage in a blender and pulse for 2 minutes or until it is finely chopped.
2. Add the watermelon and raspberries and pulse for about 1 minute or until very well combined.
3. Add the ice and blend until the smoothie is very thick and smooth.
4. Pour into 2 glasses and serve.

Per Serving

calories: 50 | fat: 0g | carbs: 11.1g | phosphorus: 31mg | potassium: 200mg
sodium: 5mg | protein: 1.1g

Golden Blueberry Scones

Prep time: 20 minutes | Cook time: 25 minutes | Serves 8

- 2 cups gluten-free flour mix or blend
- ¼ cup brown sugar
- 2 teaspoons baking powder
- ¼ teaspoon salt
- ½ cup water
- 5 tablespoons extra-virgin olive oil
- 1 large egg
- ⅔ cup fresh blueberries

1. Preheat the oven to 375ºF (190ºC). Line a baking sheet with parchment paper and set aside.
2. In a large bowl, combine the flour mix, brown sugar, baking powder, and salt and mix well.
3. In a small bowl, beat the water, olive oil, and egg until combined.
4. Add the egg mixture to the flour mixture all at once and stir, just until a dough forms. Gently work in the blueberries with your hands.
5. On the prepared baking sheet, form the mixture into an 8-inch circle. Cut into 8 wedges and separate the wedges slightly.
6. Bake the scones for 20 to 25 minutes or until light golden brown. Remove from the baking sheet and cool on a wire rack before serving.

Per Serving (1 scone)

calories: 220 | fat: 10.2g | carbs: 30.8g | phosphorus: 110mg | potassium: 170mg
sodium: 210mg | protein: 4.1g

Cranberry Almond Oats

Prep time: 5 minutes | Cook time: 0 minutes | Serves 6

- 4 cups old-fashioned rolled oats
- 2 cups unsweetened almond milk
- 2 cups water
- 1 cup dried unsweetened cranberries
- ¼ cup almond butter
- 2 teaspoons vanilla extract

1. In a medium bowl, combine the oats, almond milk, water, cranberries, almond butter, and vanilla and mix well. It's okay if the almond butter doesn't mix completely with the other ingredients. Cover tightly with plastic wrap. Refrigerate overnight, or at least 6 hours.
2. When you're ready to eat, stir the mixture and serve. You can heat it if you'd like; just put it into a saucepan and heat over low heat until the cereal is steaming.

Per Serving (¾ cup)

calories: 368 | fat: 10.1g | carbs: 61.1g | phosphorus: 286mg | potassium: 343mg
sodium: 63mg | protein: 10.1g

Pineapple and Blueberry Smoothie

Prep time: 15 minutes | Cook time: 0 minutes | Serves 2

- 1 cup frozen blueberries
- ½ cup pineapple chunks
- ½ cup English cucumber
- ½ apple
- ½ cup water

1. Put the blueberries, pineapple, cucumber, apple, and water in a blender and blend until thick and smooth.
2. Pour into 2 glasses and serve.

Per Serving

calories: 90 | fat: 1.1g | carbs: 22.1g | phosphorus: 30mg | potassium: 193mg sodium: 4mg | protein: 1.1g

Cucumber and Watercress Pita Pockets

Prep time: 15 minutes | Cook time: 5 minutes | Serves 4

- 3 eggs, beaten
- 1 scallion, both green and white parts, finely chopped
- ½ red bell pepper, finely chopped
- 2 teaspoons unsalted butter
- 1 teaspoon curry powder
- ½ teaspoon ground ginger
- 2 tablespoons light sour cream
- 2 (4-inch) plain pita bread pockets, halved
- ½ cup julienned English cucumber
- 1 cup roughly chopped watercress

1. In a small bowl, whisk together the eggs, scallion, and red pepper until well blended.
2. In a large nonstick skillet over medium heat, melt the butter.
3. Pour the egg mixture into the skillet and cook for about 3 minutes or until the eggs are just set, swirling the skillet but not stirring. Remove the eggs from the heat; set aside.
4. In a small bowl, stir together the curry powder, ginger, and sour cream until well blended.
5. Evenly divide the curry sauce among the 4 halves of the pita bread, spreading it out on one inside edge.
6. Divide the cucumber and watercress evenly between the halves.
7. Spoon the eggs into the halves, dividing the mixture evenly, to serve.

Per Serving

calories: 128 | fat: 6.8g | carbs: 10.1g | phosphorus: 110mg | potassium: 170mg sodium: 140mg | protein: 6.8g

Bell Pepper Egg Muffins

Prep time: 15 minutes | Cook time: 20 minutes | Serves 4

- Cooking spray, for greasing the muffin pans
- 4 eggs
- 2 tablespoons unsweetened rice milk
- ½ sweet onion, finely chopped
- ½ red bell pepper, finely chopped
- 1 tablespoon chopped fresh parsley
- Pinch red pepper flakes
- Pinch freshly ground black pepper

1. Preheat the oven to 350°F (180°C).
2. Spray 4 muffin pans with cooking spray; set aside.
3. In a large bowl, whisk together the eggs, milk, onion, red pepper, parsley, red pepper flakes, and black pepper until well combined.
4. Pour the egg mixture into the prepared muffin pans.
5. Bake 18 to 20 minutes or until the muffins are puffed and golden.
6. Serve warm or cold.

Per Serving

calories: 85 | fat: 5.1g | carbs: 2.8g | phosphorus: 111mg | potassium: 118mg sodium: 76mg | protein: 7.1g

Apple Cheese Wrap

Prep time: 10 minutes | Cook time: 0 minutes | Serves 2

- 2 (6-inch) flour tortillas
- 2 tablespoons plain cream cheese
- 1 apple, peeled, cored, and sliced
- thin
- 1 tablespoon honey

1. Lay both tortillas on a clean work surface and spread 1 tablespoon of cream cheese onto each tortilla, leaving about ½ inch around the edges.
2. Arrange the apple slices on the cream cheese, just off the center of the tortilla on the side closest to you, leaving about 1½ inches on each side and 2 inches on the bottom.
3. Drizzle the apples lightly with honey.
4. Fold the left and right edges of the tortillas into the center, laying the edge over the apples.
5. Taking the tortilla edge closest to you, fold it over the fruit and the side pieces. Roll the tortilla away from you, creating a snug wrap.
6. Repeat with the second tortilla.

Per Serving

calories: 190 | fat: 5.8g | carbs: 33.1g | phosphorus: 75mg | potassium: 137mg sodium: 178mg | protein: 4.1g

Easy Tacos

Prep time: 15 minutes | Cook time: 15 minutes | Serves 4

- 2 tablespoons extra-virgin olive oil
- 1½ cups frozen bell peppers
- 2 tablespoons water, divided
- 1 jalapeño pepper, minced
- 6 large eggs
- ⅛ teaspoon salt
- ⅛ teaspoon freshly ground black pepper
- 4 corn tortillas
- ½ cup shredded pepper Jack cheese

1. In a medium skillet, heat the olive oil over medium heat.
2. Add the bell peppers and stir. Add 1 tablespoon of water and cover the pan. Cook for 3 to 4 minutes, or until the vegetables are thawed and hot. Add the jalapeño pepper and cook for about 1 minute.
3. While the vegetables are cooking, in a medium bowl, combine the eggs and the remaining 1 tablespoon of water and beat well.
4. Add the eggs to the skillet and cook for 4 to 6 minutes, stirring occasionally, until the eggs are set. Sprinkle with the salt and pepper.
5. Heat the tortillas as directed on the package. Make tacos with the tortillas, egg filling, and cheese and serve.

Per Serving (1 taco)

calories: 284 | fat: 19.1g | carbs: 14.8g | phosphorus: 260mg | potassium: 263mg sodium: 253mg | protein: 13.1g

Egg-In-A-Hole

Prep time: 5 minutes | Cook time: 5 minutes | Serves 2

- 2 (½-inch-thick) slices Italian bread
- ¼ cup unsalted butter
- 2 eggs
- 2 tablespoons chopped fresh chives
- Pinch cayenne pepper
- Freshly ground black pepper, to taste

1. Using a cookie cutter or a small glass, cut a 2-inch round from the center of each piece of bread.
2. In a large nonstick skillet over medium-high heat, melt the butter.
3. Place the bread in the skillet, toast it for 1 minute, and then flip the bread over.
4. Crack the eggs into the holes the center of the bread and cook for about 2 minutes or until the eggs are set and the bread is golden brown.
5. Top with chopped chives, cayenne pepper, and black pepper.
6. Cook the bread for another 2 minutes.
7. Transfer an egg-in-the-hole to each plate to serve.

Per Serving

calories: 305 | fat: 29.1g | carbs: 12.2g | phosphorus: 120mg | potassium: 110mg sodium: 205mg | protein: 8.8g

Simple Pancake

Prep time: 15 minutes | Cook time: 20 minutes | Serves 2

- 2 eggs
- ½ cup unsweetened rice milk
- ½ cup all-purpose flour
- ¼ teaspoon ground cinnamon
- Pinch ground nutmeg
- Cooking spray, for greasing the skillet

1. Preheat the oven to 450ºF (235ºC).
2. In a medium bowl, whisk together the eggs and rice milk.
3. Stir in the flour, cinnamon, and nutmeg until blended but still slightly lumpy, but do not overmix.
4. Spray a 9-inch ovenproof skillet with cooking spray and place the skillet in the preheated oven for 5 minutes.
5. Remove the skillet carefully and pour the pancake batter into the skillet.
6. Return the skillet to the oven and bake the pancake for about 20 minutes or until it is puffed up and crispy on the edges.
7. Cut the pancake into halves to serve.

Per Serving

calories: 162 | fat: 1.1g | carbs: 29.8g | phosphorus: 75mg | potassium: 107mg
sodium: 80mg | protein: 6.8g

Bread and Rhubarb Pudding

Prep time: 15 minutes | Cook time: 50 minutes | Serves 6

- Unsalted butter, for greasing the baking dish
- 1½ cups unsweetened rice milk
- 3 eggs
- ½ cup granulated sugar
- 1 tablespoon cornstarch
- 1 vanilla bean, split
- 10 thick pieces white bread, cut into 1-inch chunks
- 2 cups chopped fresh rhubarb

1. Preheat the oven to 350ºF (180ºC).
2. Lightly grease an 8-by-8-inch baking dish with butter; set aside.
3. In a large bowl, whisk together the rice milk, eggs, sugar, and cornstarch.
4. Scrape the vanilla seeds into the milk mixture and whisk to blend.
5. Add the bread to the egg mixture and stir to completely coat the bread.
6. Add the chopped rhubarb and stir to combine.
7. Let the bread and egg mixture soak for 30 minutes.
8. Spoon the mixture into the prepared baking dish, cover with aluminum foil, and bake for 40 minutes.

9. Uncover the bread pudding and bake for an additional 10 minutes or until the pudding is golden brown and set.
10. Serve warm.

Per Serving

calories: 200 | fat: 4.2g | carbs: 35.1g | phosphorus: 110mg | potassium: 193mg
sodium: 160mg | protein: 5.9g

Summer Omelet

Prep time: 15 minutes | Cook time: 10 minutes | Serves 3

- 4 egg whites
- 1 egg
- 2 tablespoons chopped fresh parsley
- 2 tablespoons water
- Olive oil spray, for greasing the skillet
- ½ cup chopped and boiled red bell pepper
- ¼ cup chopped scallion, both green and white parts
- Freshly ground black pepper, to taste

1. In a small bowl, whisk together the egg whites, egg, parsley, and water until well blended; set aside.
2. Generously spray a large nonstick skillet with olive oil spray, and place it over medium-high heat.
3. Sauté the peppers and scallion for about 3 minutes or until softened.
4. Pour the egg mixture into the skillet over the vegetables and cook, swirling the skillet, for about 2 minutes or until the edges of the egg start to set.
5. Lift up the set edges and tilt the pan so that the uncooked egg can flow underneath the cooked egg.
6. Continue lifting and cooking the egg for about 4 minutes or until the omelet is set.
7. Loosen the omelet with a spatula and fold it in half. Cut the folded omelet into 3 portions and transfer the omelets to serving plates.
8. Season with black pepper and serve.

Per Serving

calories: 80 | fat: 3.2g | carbs: 1.9g | phosphorus: 68mg | potassium: 195mg
sodium: 230mg | protein: 12.1g

CHAPTER 4

VEGAN AND VEGETABLE

Carrot Soup

Prep time: 15 minutes | Cook time: 25 minutes | Serves 4

- 1 tablespoon olive oil
- ½ sweet onion, chopped
- 2 teaspoons grated peeled fresh ginger
- 1 teaspoon minced fresh garlic
- 4 cups water
- 3 carrots, chopped
- 1 teaspoon ground turmeric
- ½ cup coconut milk
- 1 tablespoon chopped fresh cilantro

1. In a large saucepan over medium-high heat, heat the olive oil.
2. Sauté the onion, ginger, and garlic until softened, about 3 minutes.
3. Stir in the water, carrots, and turmeric. Bring the soup to a boil, reduce the heat to low, and simmer until the carrots are tender, about 20 minutes.
4. Transfer the soup in batches to a food processor (or blender), and process with the coconut milk until the soup is smooth. Return the soup to the pan and reheat.
5. Serve topped with the cilantro.

Per Serving

calories: 115 | fat: 10.1g | carbs: 7.1g | phosphorus: 51mg | potassium: 201mg
sodium: 32mg | protein: 1.2g

Carrot and Mushroom Bisque

Prep time: 15 minutes | Cook time: 30 minutes | Serves 4

- 4 cups low-sodium vegetable broth
- 3 large carrots, sliced
- 1 yellow bell pepper, sliced
- 1 cup sliced button mushrooms
- ⅛ teaspoon salt
- ⅛ teaspoon freshly ground black pepper
- 1 (8-ounce / 227-g) package cream cheese, cubed

1. In a heavy saucepan, combine the broth, carrots, bell pepper, mushrooms, salt, and pepper over medium heat. Bring to a boil, then reduce the heat to low.
2. Simmer for 20 to 25 minutes, or until the vegetables are very tender.
3. Using a slotted spoon, remove the vegetables from the broth and transfer them to a food processor. Add the cream cheese and process until smooth.
4. Return the pureed mixture to the broth in the saucepan and stir. Reheat for 3 to 5 minutes, until steaming. Do not boil. Serve.

Per Serving

calories: 250 | fat: 20.1g | carbs: 14.1g | phosphorus: 110mg | potassium: 387mg
sodium: 430mg | protein: 4.8g

Roasted Peach Sandwich

Prep time: 5 minutes | Cook time: 15 minutes | Serves 4

- 2 fresh peaches, peeled and sliced
- 1 tablespoon extra-virgin olive oil
- 1 tablespoon freshly squeezed lemon juice
- ⅛ teaspoon salt
- ⅛ teaspoon freshly ground black
- pepper
- 4 ounces (113 g) cream cheese, at room temperature
- 2 teaspoons fresh thyme leaves
- 4 whole-wheat sourdough bread slices

1. Preheat the oven to 400ºF (205ºC).
2. Arrange the peaches on a rimmed baking sheet. Brush them with the olive oil on both sides.
3. Roast the peaches for 10 to 15 minutes, until they are light golden brown around the edges. Sprinkle with the lemon juice, salt, and pepper.
4. In a small bowl, combine the cream cheese and thyme and mix well.
5. Toast the bread and spread with the cream cheese mixture. Top with the peaches and serve.

Per Serving

calories: 252 | fat: 13.1g | carbs: 28.1g | phosphorus: 164mg | potassium: 261mg sodium: 377mg | protein: 5.9g

Arugula and Walnut Pesto Pasta

Prep time: 10 minutes | Cook time: 10 minutes | Serves 4

- 8 ounces (227 g) linguine noodles
- 2 cups packed basil leaves
- 2 cups packed arugula leaves
- ⅓ cup walnut pieces
- 3 garlic cloves
- ¼ cup extra-virgin olive oil
- Freshly ground black pepper, to taste

1. Fill a medium stockpot halfway with water, and bring to a boil. Cook the noodles al dente, and drain.
2. In a food processor, add the basil, arugula, walnuts, and garlic. Process until coarsely ground. With the food processor running, slowly add the olive oil, and continue to mix until creamy. Season with pepper.
3. Toss the noodles with the pesto and serve.

Per Serving

calories: 395 | fat: 21.2g | carbs: 0g | phosphorus: 55mg | potassium: 150mg sodium: 5mg | protein: 9.8g

Red Coleslaw

Prep time: 10 minutes | Cook time: 0 minutes | Serves 4

- 3 cups shredded red cabbage
- ½ cup shredded carrots
- ¼ cup finely chopped scallions
- Juice of 2 lemons
- 1 tablespoon honey
- 1 tablespoon extra-virgin olive oil
- 1 large tart apple, peeled and finely diced
- Freshly ground black pepper, to taste

1. In a large bowl, add the cabbage, carrots, scallions, lemon juice, honey, olive oil, and apple. Mix well and refrigerate for 30 minutes to chill. Toss with black pepper right before serving.

Per Serving

calories: 95 | fat: 4.1g | carbs: 16.1g | phosphorus: 29mg | potassium: 304mg
sodium: 282mg | protein: 1.8g

Cabbage Quiche

Prep time: 10 minutes | Cook time: 40 minutes | Serves 6

- Olive oil cooking spray
- 2 tablespoons extra-virgin olive oil
- 3 cups coleslaw blend with carrots
- 3 large eggs, beaten
- 3 large egg whites, beaten
- ½ cup half-and-half
- 1 teaspoon dried dill weed
- ⅛ teaspoon salt
- ⅛ teaspoon freshly ground black pepper
- 1 cup grated Swiss cheese

1. Preheat the oven to 350ºF (180ºC). Spray a 9-inch pie plate with cooking spray and set aside.
2. In a large skillet, heat the olive oil over medium heat. Add the coleslaw mix and cook for 4 to 6 minutes, stirring, until the cabbage is tender. Transfer the vegetables from the pan to a medium bowl to cool.
3. Meanwhile, in another medium bowl, combine the eggs and egg whites, half-and-half, dill, salt, and pepper and beat to combine.
4. Stir the cabbage mixture into the egg mixture and pour into the prepared pie plate.
5. Sprinkle with the cheese.
6. Bake for 30 to 35 minutes, or until the mixture is puffed, set, and light golden brown. Let stand for 5 minutes, then slice to serve.

Per Serving

calories: 205 | fat: 16.2g | carbs: 5.1g | phosphorus: 170mg | potassium: 156mg
sodium: 322mg | protein: 11.2g

Stir-Fried Tofu and Broccoli

Prep time: 15 minutes | Cook time: 15 minutes | Serves 4

For the Sauce:
- 3 garlic cloves
- 2-inch piece ginger, peeled
- 2 tablespoons honey
- ¼ cup rice wine vinegar
- 2 tablespoons extra-virgin olive oil

For the Stir-Fry:
- 1 (14-ounce / 397-g) package extra-firm tofu
- 1 cup long-grain white rice
- 2 tablespoons extra-virgin olive oil
- 2 cups chopped broccoli
- 1 cup shredded carrots
- 3 scallions, finely chopped

To Make the Sauce

1. Combine the garlic, ginger, honey, vinegar, and olive oil in a food processor, and purée until smooth.

To Make the Stir-Fry

2. Cut the tofu into small cubes, and press the excess moisture from the tofu using paper towels, repeating several times until dry.
3. In a medium pot, cook the rice according to package directions.
4. In a large skillet over medium heat, heat the olive oil. Add the tofu to the pan in a single layer. Carefully add one quarter of the sauce to the pan and continue to cook, flipping the tofu only once or twice every 4 minutes, until it is well browned. With a slotted spoon, transfer the tofu to a plate lined with paper towels to drain.
5. Add the broccoli to the pan. Cook, covered, stirring often, until fork-tender, about 5 minutes. Add the carrots and continue to cook for an additional 3 minutes, until softened. Add the remaining sauce to the vegetables, return the tofu to the pan, and stir to mix. Garnish with scallions and serve over rice.

`Per Serving`

calories: 412 | fat: 18.1g | carbs: 51.2g | phosphorus: 223mg | potassium: 488mg
sodium: 52mg | protein: 13.2g

Cauliflower and Green Bean Biriyani

Prep time: 10 minutes | Cook time: 30 minutes | Serves 4

- 1 cup basmati rice
- 2 tablespoons olive oil or butter, divided
- ½ teaspoon curry powder
- ½ teaspoon cumin seeds
- ½ teaspoon coriander seeds
- 1¾ cups water plus ⅔ cup water, divided
- ½ sweet onion, chopped
- 2 garlic cloves, minced
- 1 teaspoon ground coriander
- ½ teaspoon ground cardamom
- ½ teaspoon ground cumin
- ¼ teaspoon ground turmeric
- 2 cups cauliflower florets
- 1 cup green beans, cut into 2-inch segments
- 1 carrot, diced
- ¼ cup chopped cilantro leaves, for garnish

1. In a small bowl, rinse the rice until the water runs clear. Drain and set aside.
2. In a medium stockpot over medium heat, heat 1 tablespoon of olive oil. Add the curry powder, cumin seeds, and coriander seeds, stirring constantly, until fragrant, about 30 seconds. Add the rice to the pot along with 1¾ cups of water. Bring to a boil, reduce the heat, cover, and simmer for 12 minutes. Turn off the heat and let steam, covered, for 10 minutes.
3. In a large skillet over medium heat, heat the remaining tablespoon of olive oil. Add the onion, and cook for 6 to 8 minutes, until tender. Add the garlic and cook for an additional minute. Add the coriander, cardamom, cumin, and turmeric to the skillet, and stirring constantly, toast until fragrant, about 1 minute. Add the cauliflower, beans, and carrots, stirring to coat, and cook for 2 to 3 minutes. Add the remaining ⅔ cup of water to the pan, cover, and cook for 7 to 10 minutes, until the vegetables are just fork-tender.
4. Add the rice to the vegetables, and stir to blend. Serve topped with cilantro leaves.

Per Serving

calories: 173 | fat: 4.1g | carbs: 30.8g | phosphorus: 41mg | potassium: 234mg
sodium: 25mg | protein: 4.2g

Cranberry and Bulgur Stuffed Spaghetti Squash

Prep time: 20 minutes | Cook time: 50 minutes | Serves 4

For the Squash:
- 2 small spaghetti squash, halved
- 1 teaspoon olive oil
- Freshly ground black pepper, to taste

For the Filling:
- 1 teaspoon olive oil
- ½ small sweet onion, finely diced
- 1 teaspoon minced garlic
- ½ cup chopped carrot
- ½ cup cranberries
- 1 teaspoon chopped fresh thyme
- ½ teaspoon ground cumin
- ½ teaspoon ground coriander
- Juice of ½ lemon
- 1 cup cooked bulgur

To Make the Squash
1. Preheat the oven to 350ºF (180ºC).
2. Line a baking sheet with parchment paper.
3. Lightly oil the cut sides of the squash, season with pepper, and place them cut-side down on the baking sheet.
4. Bake for 25 to 30 minutes or until tender. Remove the squash from the oven and flip the squash halves over.
5. Scoop out the flesh from each half, leaving about ½ inch around the edges and keeping the skin intact.
6. Place 2 cups of squash flesh in a large bowl and reserve the rest for another recipe.

To Make the Filling
1. In a medium skillet over medium heat, heat the olive oil.
2. Sauté the onion, garlic, carrot, and cranberries for 5 to 6 minutes or until softened.
3. Add the sautéed vegetables to the squash in the bowl.
4. Add the thyme, cumin, and coriander, stirring to combine.
5. Stir in the lemon juice and cooked bulgur until well mixed.
6. Spoon the filling evenly into the squash halves.
7. Bake in the oven for about 15 minutes or until heated through.
8. Serve warm.

`Per Serving`

calories: 112 | fat: 1.9g | carbs: 16.8g | phosphorus: 40mg | potassium: 183mg sodium: 23mg | protein: 3.1g

Roasted Summer Squash Sandwiches

Prep time: 20 minutes | Cook time: 35 minutes | Serves 6

- 3 bell peppers, assorted colors, sliced
- 1 cup sliced yellow summer squash
- 1 red onion, sliced
- 2 tablespoons extra-virgin olive oil
- 2 tablespoons balsamic vinegar
- ⅛ teaspoon salt
- ⅛ teaspoon freshly ground black pepper
- 3 large whole-wheat pita breads, halved

1. Preheat the oven to 400ºF (205ºC). Line a rimmed baking sheet with parchment paper.
2. Spread the bell peppers, squash, and onion on the prepared baking sheet. Sprinkle with the olive oil, vinegar, salt, and pepper.
3. Roast for 30 to 40 minutes, turning the vegetables with a spatula once during cooking, until they are tender and light golden brown.
4. Pile the vegetables into the pita breads and serve.

Per Serving

calories: 185 | fat: 5.1g | carbs: 31.2g | phosphorus: 107mg | potassium: 290mg
sodium: 235mg | protein: 5.1g

Alfredo Lasagna Spinach Rolls

Prep time: 25 minutes | Cook time: 50 minutes | Serves 4

- 4 whole-grain lasagna noodles
- 2 tablespoons extra-virgin olive oil
- 1 large onion, chopped
- 2 cups frozen whole-leaf spinach, thawed (measure while frozen)
- 1 (8-ounce / 227-g) package cream cheese, at room temperature, divided
- ⅓ cup shredded Parmesan cheese

1. Bring a large pot of water to a boil over high heat and add the lasagna noodles. Simmer for 8 to 9 minutes or until the pasta is almost al dente but still has a thin white line in the center. Drain, reserving ¼ cup of the pasta water, and set aside.
2. Meanwhile, in a saucepan, heat the olive oil over medium heat. Add the onions and cook for 6 to 8 minutes, stirring, until the onions are tender and starting to turn brown.
3. While the onions are cooking, drain the spinach and put the leaves into some paper towels. Squeeze well to remove most of the water from the spinach.
4. Add the spinach to the onions, stir, and turn off the heat. Add 6 ounces (170 g) of cream cheese to the vegetables and stir until combined. Set aside.

5. In a small saucepan, combine the remaining 2 ounces (57 g) of cream cheese with the reserved pasta water. Heat over low heat, stirring often with a wire whisk, until smooth.
6. In a 9-inch baking dish, place 2 tablespoons of the cream cheese sauce.
7. On a work surface, place the lasagna noodles. Divide the spinach mixture among them and roll them up.
8. Place the rolls, seam-side down, on the sauce in the casserole. Top with the remaining sauce.
9. Sprinkle the lasagna rolls with the Parmesan cheese. Bake for 25 to 35 minutes, or until the lasagna is bubbling and the top starts to brown.

Per Serving

calories: 389 | fat: 24.1g | carbs: 34.1g | phosphorus: 120mg | potassium: 380mg
sodium: 412mg | protein: 12.8g

Pasta Fasul

Prep time: 25 minutes | Cook time: 25 minutes | Serves 6

- 1 (15-ounce / 425-g) can low-sodium great northern beans, drained and rinsed, divided
- 2 cups frozen peppers and onions, thawed, divided
- 5 cups low-sodium vegetable broth
- ⅛ teaspoon salt
- ⅛ teaspoon freshly ground black pepper
- 1 cup whole-grain orecchiette pasta
- 2 tablespoons extra-virgin olive oil
- ⅓ cup grated Parmesan cheese

1. In a large saucepan, place the beans and cover with water. Bring to a boil over high heat and boil for 10 minutes. Drain the beans.
2. In a food processor or blender, combine ⅓ cup of beans and ⅓ cup of thawed peppers and onions. Process until smooth.
3. In the same saucepan, combine the pureed mixture, the remaining 1⅔ cups of peppers and onions, the remaining beans, the broth, and the salt and pepper and bring to a simmer.
4. Add the pasta to the saucepan and stir. Bring to a boil, reduce the heat to low, and simmer for 8 to 10 minutes, or until the pasta is tender.
5. Serve drizzled with olive oil and topped with Parmesan cheese.

Per Serving

calories: 246 | fat: 7.1g | carbs: 36.1g | phosphorus: 190mg | potassium: 593mg
sodium: 270mg | protein: 12.2g

Brown Rice Stuffed Bell Peppers

Prep time: 20 minutes | Cook time: 65 minutes | Serves 4

- 6 red bell peppers
- 2 tablespoons extra-virgin olive oil
- 1 onion, chopped
- ½ teaspoon Italian seasoning
- ⅛ teaspoon salt
- ⅛ teaspoon freshly ground black pepper
- 2 cups cooked brown rice
- ⅔ cup shredded pepper Jack cheese

1. Cut the top inch off of 4 peppers. Then use a knife and your fingers to remove the seeds and light-colored membranes from the inside of the peppers and set aside. Be careful so you don't split the peppers or cut a hole in the bottom.
2. Seed and chop the remaining 2 bell peppers.
3. Preheat the oven to 375°F (190°C).
4. In a large saucepan, heat the olive oil over medium heat. Add the onion and cook for about 3 minutes, stirring, until crisp-tender.
5. Add the chopped bell peppers. Sprinkle with the Italian seasoning, salt, and pepper. Cook and stir for 3 to 5 minutes or until crisp tender. Stir in the brown rice and remove from the heat.
6. Stir the cheese into the vegetable mixture.
7. Place the bell peppers into a casserole dish so they fit snugly. Fill each pepper with the vegetable mixture.
8. Pour ½ cup of water into the casserole dish, around the bell peppers. Cover the dish with aluminum foil.
9. Bake for 35 minutes, then remove the foil. Bake for another 20 to 25 minutes or until the peppers are tender and the filling is brown on top.

Per Serving

calories: 317 | fat: 14.2g | carbs: 40.1g | phosphorus: 250mg | potassium: 581mg
sodium: 203mg | protein: 8.9g

Spinach and Falafel Tortillas

Prep time: 10 minutes | Cook time: 15 minutes | Serves 4

- 6 ounces (170 g) baby spinach
- 1 (15-ounce / 425-g) can chickpeas, drained and rinsed
- 2 teaspoons ground cumin
- ¾ cup flour
- 2 tablespoons canola oil, divided, for frying
- ¼ cup plain, unsweetened yogurt
- 2 garlic cloves, minced
- Juice of 1 lemon
- Freshly ground black pepper, to taste
- 4 tortillas
- 1 cucumber, cut into spears
- 2 slices red onion
- Salad greens, for serving

1. Place the spinach in a colander in the sink, and pour boiling water over it to wilt the spinach. Allow it to cool, then press as much water out of the spinach as possible.
2. In a food processor, add the spinach, chickpeas, cumin, and flour. Pulse until just blended.
3. Divide the mixture into tablespoon-size balls, and use your hands to press them flat into patties.
4. In a large skillet over medium-high heat, heat 1 tablespoon of oil. Add half of the falafel patties, and cook for 2 to 3 minutes on each side, until browned and crisp. Repeat with the remaining falafel patties.
5. In a small bowl, combine the yogurt, garlic, lemon juice, and pepper.
6. On each tortilla, place 3 falafel patties, a couple cucumber spears, a few red-onion rings, and a handful of salad greens. Top each with 1 tablespoon of the yogurt sauce.

Per Serving

calories: 242 | fat: 7.1g | carbs: 36.8g | phosphorus: 111mg | potassium: 246mg sodium: 286mg | protein: 7.8g

Bulgur and Bean Stuffed Delicata Squash

Prep time: 10 minutes | Cook time: 35 minutes | Serves 4

- 2 small delicata squash, halved lengthwise and seeded
- 6 teaspoons extra-virgin olive oil, divided
- 1 cup bulgur
- ½ sweet onion, diced

- 2 tablespoons chili powder
- 1 cup canned black beans, drained and rinsed
- ½ cup frozen or fresh corn kernels
- 2 scallions, thinly sliced, for garnish

1. Preheat the oven to 425ºF (220ºC).
2. Brush the cut squash with 2 teaspoons of olive oil and place cut-side down on a baking sheet. Cook for 25 to 30 minutes, until the flesh is tender.
3. Meanwhile, in a saucepan, bring the bulgur and 2 cups of water to a boil. Reduce the heat, cover, and simmer for 12 to 15 minutes, until the liquid is absorbed. Drain well.
4. In a large skillet, heat the remaining 4 teaspoons of olive oil over medium heat. Cook the onion for 4 to 5 minutes, until it just starts to brown. Stir in the chili powder, black beans, and corn. Stir in the bulgur, and cook for an additional minute.
5. Divide the filling between the squash halves, sprinkle with scallions, and serve.

Per Serving

calories: 315 | fat: 7.9g | carbs: 55.8g | phosphorus: 235mg | potassium: 811mg sodium: 310mg | protein: 9.8g

Roasted Eggplan and Zucchini Barley Bowl

Prep time: 10 minutes | Cook time: 30 minutes | Serves 4

- 2 small Asian eggplants, diced
- 2 small zucchinis, diced
- ½ red bell pepper, chopped
- ½ sweet onion, cut into wedges
- 2 tablespoons extra-virgin olive oil, divided
- Freshly ground black pepper, to taste
- 1 cup barley
- Juice of 1 lemon
- 3 garlic cloves, minced
- ¼ cup basil leaves, roughly chopped
- ¼ cup crumbled feta cheese
- 2 cups arugula or mixed baby salad greens

1. Preheat the oven to 425ºF (220ºC).
2. In a medium bowl, toss the eggplant, zucchini, bell pepper, and onion with 1 tablespoon of olive oil, and arrange the vegetables in a single layer on a baking sheet. Season with pepper.
3. Roast the vegetables for about 25 minutes, stirring once or twice, until they are browned and tender. Set aside.
4. Meanwhile, in a medium pot, add the barley and 2 cups of water. Bring to a boil, reduce the heat to simmer, cover, and cook for 20 minutes. Turn off the heat, and let rest for 10 minutes. Fluff with a fork, and drain any remaining water.
5. In a small bowl, whisk the lemon juice, garlic, and remaining tablespoon of olive oil.
6. Toss the vegetables with the barley, and then mix together with the lemon-garlic dressing. Right before serving, stir in the basil, feta cheese, and salad greens.

Per Serving

calories: 293 | fat: 10.1g | carbs: 43.8g | phosphorus: 200mg | potassium: 544mg
sodium: 120mg | protein: 8.8g

Slow Cooked Kidney Bean Chili

Prep time: 20 minutes | Cook time: 8 hours | Serves 6

- 1 cup dried kidney beans, sorted and rinsed
- 6 cups low-sodium vegetable broth
- 1 yellow onion, chopped
- 4 garlic cloves, minced
- 2 tablespoons chili powder
- ⅛ teaspoon salt
- ⅛ teaspoon freshly ground black pepper
- 2 tablespoons extra-virgin olive oil

1. In a large saucepan, cover the beans with water and bring to a boil. Boil for 10 minutes. Drain the beans, discarding the water.

2. In a slow cooker, combine the beans, broth, onion, garlic, chili powder, salt, and pepper.
3. Cover and cook on low for 6 to 8 hours or on high for 3 to 4 hours, or until the beans and rice are tender.
4. Transfer ½ cup of the beans from the slow cooker to a food processor or blender. Add the olive oil and puree. Return to the slow cooker. Heat on high for 20 minutes, then serve.

calories: 172 | fat: 5.1g | carbs: 24.1g | phosphorus: 150mg | potassium: 562mg
sodium: 272mg | protein: 8.1g

Collard Stuffed Peppers

Prep time: 10 minutes | Cook time: 50 minutes | Serves 4

- 2 medium red bell peppers
- 2 tablespoons extra-virgin olive oil, divided
- Freshly ground black pepper, to taste
- 6 cups loosely packed collard greens, trimmed
- ½ sweet onion, chopped
- 3 garlic cloves, minced
- 1 cup cooked white rice
- Juice of 1 lemon
- ¼ cup toasted sunflower seeds, divided

1. Preheat the oven to 400ºF (205ºC).
2. Halve the peppers through the stems, and remove the seeds and stems. Brush the inside and outside of the peppers with 1 tablespoon of olive oil and season with the pepper. Place the peppers cut-side down in a baking dish. Bake for 10 to 15 minutes, until just tender. Remove from the oven and flip the peppers cut-side up. Set aside, leaving the oven on.
3. In a large saucepan, bring 4 cups of water to a boil. Add the collard greens and cook until just tender, 5 to 7 minutes. Drain and rinse under cold water. Chop finely.
4. In a large skillet, heat the remaining tablespoon of olive oil over medium heat. Add the onion, and cook, stirring often, for 5 to 7 minutes, until it begins to brown. Add the garlic and cook until fragrant. Stir in the collard greens. Remove from the heat, and stir in the rice and lemon juice. Season with pepper.
5. Divide the filling between the pepper halves and top each pepper half with 1 tablespoon of the sunflower seeds. Add ¼ cup of water to the baking dish, cover with aluminum foil, and bake for 20 minutes, until heated through. Uncover and bake for an additional 5 minutes.

calories: 305 | fat: 9.1g | carbs: 49.8g | phosphorus: 150mg | potassium: 400mg
sodium: 21mg | protein: 8.2g

CHAPTER 5

POULTRY

Thai Chicken and Cabbage Salad

Prep time: 10 minutes | Cook time: 0 minutes | Serves 6

- 3 cups shredded cooked chicken (about 1 pound / 454 g)
- 1 (10-ounce / 283-g) package shredded cabbage with carrots
- 2 limes
- 1/3 cup extra-virgin olive oil
- 1/4 cup peanut butter
- 1/4 teaspoon freshly ground black pepper
- 1/4 cup chopped peanuts

1. In a large bowl, combine the chicken and cabbage and toss to mix.
2. In a small bowl, zest one of the limes. Juice both of the limes into the bowl. Add the olive oil, peanut butter, and pepper and mix with a whisk.
3. Drizzle the dressing over the salad and toss. Top with the peanuts and serve.

Per Serving

calories: 416 | fat: 30.8g | carbs: 8.8g | phosphorus: 240mg | potassium: 409mg
sodium: 120mg | protein: 27.9g

Vietnamese Turkey and Cabbage Pho

Prep time: 10 minutes | Cook time: 20 minutes | Serves 4

- 1 tablespoon olive oil
- 1/2 pound (227 g) ground white turkey meat
- 2 cups chopped Napa cabbage
- 1 large carrot, peeled and thinly sliced
- 3 scallions, white and green parts, chopped
- 2 garlic cloves, minced
- 1 teaspoon ground ginger
- 1/4 teaspoon ground cloves
- 5 cups water
- 4 ounces (113 g) dry rice noodles
- 1 tablespoon freshly squeezed lime juice

1. In a large pot, heat the oil over medium heat.
2. Add the ground turkey, cabbage, carrots, scallions, and garlic. Sauté for 4 to 5 minutes or until the turkey is browned.
3. Add the ginger, cloves, and water and bring to a simmer.
4. Reduce the heat to low and simmer 5 minutes.
5. Stir in the rice noodles and remove the pot from the heat; cover and let stand for 10 minutes or until the noodles are soft.
6. Stir in the lime juice and serve immediately.

Per Serving

calories: 283 | fat: 9.8g | carbs: 28.8g | phosphorus: 216mg | potassium: 356mg
sodium: 127mg | protein: 17.8g

Marinated Onion Chicken

Prep time: 10 minutes | Cook time: 30 minutes | Serves 4

- ½ cup chopped sweet onion
- ¼ cup olive oil
- 2 tablespoons freshly squeezed lemon juice
- 1 tablespoon chopped fresh oregano
- 1 teaspoon minced garlic
- 1 teaspoon smoked paprika
- 4 (3-ounce / 85-g) boneless skinless chicken thighs

1. In a blender, add the onion, olive oil, lemon juice, oregano, garlic, and paprika and purée.
2. Pour into a large resealable plastic bag, and add the chicken thighs.
3. Press the air out of the bag, seal, and place in the refrigerator so the chicken can marinate for 2 hours, turning it several times.
4. Preheat the oven to 400ºF (205ºC).
5. Place the chicken in a baking dish, and discard the remaining marinade.
6. Roast the chicken until it is cooked through, about 30 minutes.
7. Serve hot.

Per Serving

calories: 155 | fat: 8.1g | carbs: 0g | phosphorus: 166mg | potassium: 223mg
sodium: 56mg | protein: 19.1g

Slow Cooked Apple Chicken

Prep time: 15 minutes | Cook time: 6 hours | Serves 4

- 1 large yellow onion, chopped
- 6 boneless skinless chicken thighs, cut into strips
- 3 Granny Smith apples, sliced
- 2 tablespoons Dijon mustard
- 2 tablespoons honey
- ⅛ teaspoon salt
- ⅛ teaspoon freshly ground black pepper

1. In a slow cooker, place the onions. Top with the chicken, then the apples.
2. In a small bowl, combine the mustard, honey, salt, and pepper and mix well. Pour the mixture over the ingredients in the slow cooker.
3. Cover and cook on low for 6 hours or on high for 3 hours, or until the chicken is cooked through and the apples and onions are tender. Serve.

Per Serving

calories: 310 | fat: 6.8g | carbs: 30.1g | phosphorus: 260mg | potassium: 466mg
sodium: 370mg | protein: 29.8g

Chicken and Carrot Patties

Prep time: 25 minutes | Cook time: 20 minutes | Serves 4

- 3 tablespoons extra-virgin olive oil, divided
- 1 large carrot, finely grated or diced
- 1 yellow onion, grated or diced
- ½ cup puffed rice cereal, crushed
- 1 teaspoon dried dill weed
- Pinch salt
- ⅛ teaspoon freshly ground black pepper
- 1 pound (454 g) lean ground chicken

1. In a large skillet, heat 1 tablespoon of olive oil over medium heat.
2. Add the carrot and onion and cook for 4 to 6 minutes, until tender. Add the crushed cereal, dill, salt, and pepper and stir. Transfer the vegetable mixture into a medium bowl and let cool for 15 minutes. Do not wipe out or wash the skillet.
3. Add the ground chicken to the vegetables and work gently but thoroughly with your hands until combined.
4. Form the chicken mixture into 4 patties and place onto a plate and freeze for 10 minutes, so they firm up and are easier to work with.
5. In the same skillet, heat the remaining 2 tablespoons of olive oil over medium heat. Add the chicken patties; cook for 6 to 7 minutes per side, turning once, until the patties reach 165ºF (74ºC) and the juices run clear. Serve.

Per Serving

calories: 312 | fat: 14.8g | carbs: 5.9g | phosphorus: 263mg | potassium: 388mg
sodium: 141mg | protein: 35.8g

Apricot Chicken with Green Beans

Prep time: 15 minutes | Cook time: 15 minutes | Serves 4

- 1 (15-ounce / 425-g) can canned apricot halves, strained, reserving juice, divided
- 12 ounces (340 g) boneless skinless chicken breasts, cubed
- ⅛ teaspoon salt
- ⅛ teaspoon freshly ground black pepper
- 2 tablespoons extra-virgin olive oil
- 1 yellow onion, chopped
- 1 cup green beans

1. In a food processor or blender, combine four apricot halves with the juice from the can; process until smooth and set aside.
2. Sprinkle the chicken with salt and pepper.
3. In a large skillet, heat the olive oil over medium heat and add the chicken; cook until lightly browned, stirring occasionally for 3 to 5 minutes. Remove the chicken from the skillet and set aside.

4. Add the onion to the skillet; cook and stir for 3 to 4 minutes or until crisp-tender. Add the green beans to the skillet; cook and stir for another 3 minutes, until crisp-tender.
5. Return the chicken to the skillet and add the apricot sauce mixture. Bring to a simmer and simmer for 4 to 6 minutes or until the chicken is cooked through.
6. Add the remaining apricots to the skillet and heat through. Serve.

Per Serving

calories: 255 | fat: 9.8g | carbs: 16.8g | phosphorus: 255mg | potassium: 600mg
sodium: 128mg | protein: 26.8g

Chicken Pot Pie

Prep time: 15 minutes | Cook time: 45 minutes | Serves 6

- 3 tablespoons unsalted butter
- ½ small sweet onion, chopped
- 2 teaspoons minced garlic
- 3 tablespoons all-purpose flour
- 1 cup sodium-free chicken stock
- 1 teaspoon chopped fresh thyme
- Freshly ground black pepper, to taste
- 1 carrot, diced
- ½ sweet potato, peeled and diced
- 2 cups chopped cooked chicken breast
- ½ cup frozen peas
- 1 store-bought 9-inch pie shell

1. Preheat the oven to 425ºF (220ºC).
2. In a large saucepan over medium-high heat, melt the butter.
3. Add the onion and garlic, and sauté until softened, about 3 minutes.
4. Whisk in the flour to form a paste, and cook for 1 minute.
5. Whisk in the chicken stock, and cook until the sauce thickens, about 6 minutes.
6. Whisk in the thyme, and season the sauce with pepper.
7. Remove the sauce from the heat and set it aside.
8. In a medium saucepan of boiling water, add the carrot and sweet potato, and cook until tender, about 6 minutes. Drain, and add the vegetables to the sauce.
9. Add the chicken and peas to the sauce, and stir to combine. Spoon the chicken mixture into a 9-inch casserole dish.
10. Arrange the pie crust over the chicken mixture, cut off any excess around the edges, press the crust to the casserole dish to seal, and with a paring knife make a few slits in the crust to allow steam to escape.
11. Bake on a baking sheet until the crust is golden and the filling is bubbly, about 30 minutes.

Per Serving

calories: 267 | fat: 13.9g | carbs: 17.8g | phosphorus: 129mg | potassium: 252mg
sodium: 190mg | protein: 15.8g

Chimichurri Chicken and Pepper Kebabs

Prep time: 20 minutes | Cook time: 10 minutes | Serves 4

- 12 ounces (340 g) boneless skinless chicken breasts, cubed
- Pinch salt
- ⅛ teaspoon freshly ground black pepper
- 1 red bell pepper, cubed
- 1 yellow bell pepper, cubed
- 3 scallions, white and green parts, cut into 1-inch pieces
- ½ cup chopped flat-leaf parsley
- ¼ cup chopped cilantro
- 2 garlic cloves, minced
- 3 tablespoons extra-virgin olive oil, divided
- 1 tablespoon red wine vinegar

1. Prepare and preheat the grill to medium coals and set a grill 6 inches from the coals.
2. Sprinkle the chicken breast cubes with salt and pepper.
3. Thread the chicken, red bell pepper, yellow bell pepper, and scallions onto 8-inch metal skewers, alternating pieces of chicken with the veggies. Refrigerate.
4. In a small bowl, stir together the parsley, cilantro, garlic, 2 tablespoons olive oil, and the vinegar until well mixed.
5. Brush the kebabs with the remaining 1 tablespoon olive oil and grill, turning once, until the chicken is cooked to 165ºF (74ºC) internal temperature and the vegetables are tender, 7 to 9 minutes.
6. Place the kebabs on a serving plate and drizzle with the sauce.
7. Serve.

Per Serving

calories: 218 | fat: 13.1g | carbs: 4.8g | phosphorus: 205mg | potassium: 480mg sodium: 87mg | protein: 19.8g

Classic Tandoori Chicken

Prep time: 15 minutes | Cook time: 30 minutes | Serves 4

- 6 tablespoons plain yogurt
- 1 tablespoon freshly squeezed lemon juice
- 2 teaspoons grated peeled fresh ginger
- 2 teaspoons garam masala
- 1½ teaspoons curry powder
- 1 teaspoon honey
- 1 teaspoon minced garlic
- ½ teaspoon paprika
- Pinch cayenne pepper
- 4 (3-ounce/ 85-g) boneless skinless chicken breasts

1. In a medium bowl, whisk together the yogurt, lemon juice, ginger, garam masala, curry powder, honey, garlic, paprika, and cayenne pepper until well blended.
2. Add the chicken breasts to the bowl, and turn to coat. Cover the bowl and place it in the refrigerator for at least 1 hour, or up to 12 hours, to marinate.
3. Preheat the oven to 400°F (205°C).
4. Remove the chicken breasts from the marinade, and place them in a baking dish.
5. Bake until the chicken is cooked through, turning once, about 30 minutes.
6. Serve hot.

Per Serving

calories: 110 | fat: 1.9g | carbs: 2.1g | phosphorus: 160mg | potassium: 222mg sodium: 62mg | protein: 22.1g

Curried Turkey and Cauliflower

Prep time: 15 minutes | Cook time: 30 minutes | Serves 6

- 1 tablespoon olive oil, plus more for the baking dish
- 1 medium sweet onion, chopped
- 2 teaspoons minced garlic
- ¼ cup all-purpose flour
- 1 cup sodium-free chicken stock
- 1 cup water

- ½ cup heavy (whipping) cream
- 1 tablespoon curry powder
- 2 cups cauliflower florets
- 1 red bell pepper, diced
- 8 ounces (227 g) cooked turkey
- 2 cups cooked basmati rice

1. Preheat the oven to 400°F (205°C).
2. Lightly coat a baking dish with olive oil.
3. In a large saucepan over medium-high heat, heat 1 tablespoon of olive oil.
4. Add the onion and garlic, and sauté until softened, about 3 minutes.
5. Whisk in the flour to form a paste, and cook for 1 minute.
6. Whisk in the chicken stock, water, and cream and continue whisking until the sauce thickens, about 5 minutes.
7. Whisk in the curry powder, and remove the sauce from the heat.
8. Stir in the cauliflower, bell pepper, turkey, and rice.
9. Spoon the mixture into the prepared casserole dish. Bake until the casserole is heated through and bubbly, about 20 minutes.
10. Serve hot.

Per Serving

calories: 266 | fat: 12.8g | carbs: 23.9g | phosphorus: 160mg | potassium: 322mg sodium: 109mg | protein: 15.2g

Moroccan Chicken Stew

- 2 tablespoons olive oil
- 12 ounces (340 g) boneless skinless chicken thighs, cubed
- 1 onion, chopped
- 4 garlic cloves, minced
- 2 cups baby carrots
- 1 cup low-sodium chicken broth
- 1 teaspoon ground ginger

- 1 teaspoon ground cumin
- ½ teaspoon paprika
- ½ teaspoon ground turmeric
- Pinch salt
- ⅛ teaspoon freshly ground black pepper
- 1½ cups frozen baby peas

1. Heat the olive oil in a large skillet over medium heat.
2. Add the chicken and onion and sauté for 3 minutes or until the chicken begins to brown.
3. Stir in the garlic, carrots, and chicken broth and bring to a simmer.
4. Reduce the heat to low and stir in the ginger, cumin, paprika, turmeric, salt, and pepper. Partially cover and simmer for 6 minutes.
5. Add the peas and simmer for 2 to 4 minutes longer or until the chicken registers 165ºF (74ºC) internal temperature and the vegetables are tender-crisp.
6. Serve.

Per Serving

calories: 296 | fat: 11.1g | carbs: 17.8g | phosphorus: 266mg | potassium: 585mg
sodium: 240mg | protein: 29.8g

Italian Turkey and Mushroom Kebabs

- 2 tablespoons olive oil
- 2 tablespoons freshly squeezed lemon juice
- 2 tablespoons yellow mustard
- 1 garlic clove, minced
- 1 teaspoon dried Italian seasoning

- 1 pound (454 g) turkey tenderloin, cubed
- 16 whole small mushrooms
- 2 red bell peppers, cut into 1-inch pieces

1. Prepare and preheat the grill to medium coals and arrange the rack 6 inches from the heat.
2. In a small bowl, whisk together the olive oil, lemon juice, mustard, garlic, and Italian seasoning. Set aside.

3. Thread the turkey, mushrooms, and bell pepper onto 4 (10-inch) metal skewers, alternating meat and vegetables.
4. Place the kebabs on the rack and brush them with some of the olive oil mixture.
5. Close the grill and cook until the turkey reaches 165ºF (74ºC) internal temperature, brushing twice with the olive oil mixture and turning the kebabs occasionally.
6. Brush the kebabs with all of the remaining marinade and cook, turning frequently, for 2 minutes longer. Serve.

Per Serving

calories: 226 | fat: 8.9g | carbs: 6.9g | phosphorus: 289mg | potassium: 558mg
sodium: 220mg | protein: 28.7g

Asparagus and Turkey Risotto

Prep time: 10 minutes | Cook time: 20 minutes | Serves 6

- 4 cups low-sodium chicken broth
- 2 tablespoons olive oil
- 1 onion, chopped
- 2 garlic cloves, minced
- 1 pound (454 g) turkey tenderloin, cubed
- 1½ cups arborio rice or long-grain white rice
- 2 cups asparagus pieces
- 2 tablespoons unsalted butter
- 2 tablespoons grated Parmesan cheese

1. In a small saucepan over low heat, pour the broth and bring to a simmer.
2. Heat the oil in a large saucepan over medium heat.
3. Sauté the onion and garlic for 2 minutes.
4. Add the turkey and rice and sauté 2 more minutes.
5. Start adding the broth to the rice mixture, about ½ cup at a time, stirring constantly.
6. When the broth is absorbed, add more broth. You can stir less often as the rice begins to cook, but keep an eye on the pan.
7. After 15 minutes, add the asparagus to the rice mixture. Continue cooking and adding more broth.
8. The risotto is done when the rice is tender, and most of the broth is absorbed. This whole process should take about 20 minutes. You may not need all of the broth. This dish can be soupier or thicker, depending on how much broth you add and your taste.
9. Stir in the butter and cheese and serve immediately.

Per Serving

calories: 381 | fat: 10.8g | carbs: 42.9g | phosphorus: 300mg | potassium: 500mg
sodium: 176mg | protein: 25.8g

Crispy Chicken

Prep time: 15 minutes | Cook time: 30 minutes | Serves 4

- ½ cup all-purpose flour
- 2 eggs, beaten
- ½ cup Italian seasoned bread crumbs
- ¼ teaspoon smoked paprika
- 12 ounces (340 g) boneless skinless chicken thighs
- Pinch freshly ground pepper
- Olive oil cooking spray

1. Preheat the oven to 350ºF (180ºC).
2. Place the flour on a plate, the eggs in a shallow bowl, and the bread crumbs and paprika on another plate. Line the three dishes in a row.
3. Season a piece of chicken with pepper, and dredge it first in the flour, then the egg, then the bread crumbs until the chicken is completely coated. Repeat for the remaining chicken.
4. Arrange the chicken on a baking sheet, and coat lightly with cooking spray.
5. Bake until the chicken is cooked through, browned, and crispy, about 30 minutes.
6. Serve hot.

Per Serving

calories: 245 | fat: 6.9g | carbs: 21.8g | phosphorus: 220mg | potassium: 260mg
sodium: 205mg | protein: 22.8g

Tunisian Chicken Thighs with Rice

Prep time: 10 minutes | Cook time: 40 minutes | Serves 4

- 1 tablespoon olive oil
- 12 ounces (340 g) boneless skinless chicken thighs
- ¼ small sweet onion, chopped
- 1 tablespoon grated peeled fresh ginger
- 2 teaspoons minced garlic
- 1 teaspoon paprika
- 1 teaspoon ground coriander
- ½ teaspoon ground cumin
- ¼ teaspoon ground turmeric
- ¼ teaspoon ground allspice
- ¾ cup basmati rice
- 1½ cups water
- 2 tablespoons chopped fresh cilantro

1. In a large skillet over medium-high heat, heat the olive oil.
2. Add the chicken and brown on both sides, about 6 minutes total. Transfer to a plate.
3. In the skillet, add the onion, ginger, and garlic and sauté until softened, about 3 minutes.

4. Stir in the paprika, coriander, cumin, turmeric, allspice, and rice and mix well to coat the rice with the spices.
5. Add the water and the chicken, and bring the mixture to a boil. Reduce the heat to low, cover the skillet, and simmer until the liquid is absorbed and the chicken is cooked through, about 30 minutes.
6. Garnish with the cilantro, and serve hot.

Per Serving

calories: 266 | fat: 6.8g | carbs: 28.8g | phosphorus: 190mg | potassium: 265mg sodium: 75mg | protein: 19.1g

Creamy Cider Chicken

Prep time: 5 minutes | Cook time: 25 minutes | Serves 8

- 4 bone-in chicken breasts
- 2 tablespoons lightly salted butter
- ¾ cup apple cider vinegar
- ²/₃ cup unsweetened coconut milk or

cream
- Kosher salt and ground black pepper, to taste

1. Melt the butter in a skillet over medium heat.
2. Season the chicken with the pepper and add to the skillet. Cook over low heat for about 20 minutes.
3. Remove the chicken from the heat and set aside in a dish.
4. In the same skillet, add the cider and bring to a boil until most of it has evaporated.
5. Add the coconut cream and let cook for 1 minute until slightly thickened.
6. Pour the cider cream over the cooked chicken and serve.

Per Serving

calories: 87 | fat: 8.2g | carbs: 1.9g | phosphorus: 37mg | potassium: 75mg sodium: 94mg | protein: 1.6g

Chicken and Vegetable Casserole

- 2 tablespoons extra-virgin olive oil
- 6 bone-in skin-on chicken thighs
- 1 yellow onion, chopped
- 2½ cups plus ⅓ cup water
- ¼ teaspoon salt
- 3 cups frozen mixed vegetables
- 3 tablespoons flour
- ⅛ teaspoon freshly ground black pepper
- 1 cup crushed crisp rice cereal

1. In a large saucepan, heat the olive oil over medium heat.
2. Add the chicken thighs, skin-side down. Brown the skin thoroughly, moving the chicken around from time to time when it no longer sticks to the pan. This should take 12 to 15 minutes.
3. Remove the chicken from the skillet. Add the onion; cook and stir for 2 minutes to loosen the pan drippings.
4. Return the chicken to the skillet and add 2½ cups of water and the salt. Bring to a simmer, then reduce the heat to low and simmer for 30 to 40 minutes, stirring occasionally, until the chicken reaches 165ºF (74ºC) and the juices run clear.
5. Remove the chicken from the saucepan and let cool for 10 minutes, while keeping the broth simmering. Then remove the meat from the skin and bones. Discard the skin and bones; shred the meat and return to the saucepan.
6. Add the frozen vegetables and bring to a simmer. Simmer for 3 to 5 minutes, stirring occasionally, or until the vegetables are thawed.
7. Combine the flour with the remaining ⅓ cup of water and pepper; mix well. Stir into the saucepan and simmer for 3 to 5 minutes or until the sauce has thickened.
8. Preheat the oven to 400ºF (205ºC).
9. Pour the chicken mixture into a 2-quart baking dish and top with the cereal.
10. Bake for 20 to 25 minutes, or until the filling is bubbling and the cereal is lightly browned. Serve.

Per Serving

calories: 204 | fat: 8.9g | carbs: 8.9g | phosphorus: 180mg | potassium: 265mg sodium: 182mg | protein: 20.8g

CHAPTER 6

BEEF LAMB AND PORK

Beef Hamburgers

Prep time: 15 minutes | Cook time: 15 minutes | Serves 4

- 12 ounces (340 g) lean ground beef
- ½ cup chopped sweet onion
- 1 teaspoon minced fresh garlic
- 1 teaspoon Dijon mustard
- ½ teaspoon chopped fresh thyme
- Pinch freshly ground black pepper
- 1 tablespoon olive oil

1. In a large bowl, mix together the beef, onion, garlic, mustard, thyme, and pepper until well combined.
2. Divide the meat mixture into 4 equal balls, and form into ½-inch-thick patties.
3. In a large skillet over medium-high heat, heat the olive oil.
4. Pan-fry the burgers until they are cooked through and browned, about 6 minutes per side.
5. Serve hot.

Per Serving

calories: 151 | fat: 8.1g | carbs: 1.1g | phosphorus: 162mg | potassium: 300mg sodium: 71mg | protein: 17.9g

Roasted Pork and Grapes

Prep time: 20 minutes | Cook time: 25 minutes | Serves 4

- 2 tablespoons extra-virgin olive oil
- 1 chopped red onion
- 2 pears, seeded and cut into ½-inch wedges
- 1 (12-ounce / 340-g) pork tenderloin, cut into 1-inch strips
- ⅛ teaspoon salt
- ⅛ teaspoon freshly ground black pepper
- 1½ cups red grapes
- 1 teaspoon dried thyme leaves

1. Preheat the oven to 400ºF (205ºC).
2. Drizzle the olive oil onto a rimmed baking sheet. Add the onion and pears; toss to coat. Roast for 10 minutes.
3. Remove the pan from the oven and add the pork. Sprinkle with the salt and pepper. Add the grapes and sprinkle everything with the thyme; stir gently.
4. Arrange the fruit and pork in a single layer.
5. Roast, uncovered, stirring gently once during cooking time, for 13 to 18 minutes or until the fruit is tender and the pork registers at least 145ºF (63ºC) with a food thermometer. Stir and serve.

Per Serving

calories: 284 | fat: 10.2g | carbs: 26.8g | phosphorus: 260mg | potassium: 610mg sodium: 130mg | protein: 22.9g

Beef Enchiladas

- 1 pound (454 g) ground lean beef
- ½ cup shallots, chopped
- 1 clove of garlic
- 1 teaspoon ground cumin
- ½ teaspoon cayenne pepper
- 1 (7-ounce / 198-g) can enchilada sauce
- 12 corn tortillas
- A bit of low extra cheese on top (optional)
- Kosher salt and ground black pepper, to taste

1. In a medium frying pan with 1 teaspoon of oil, brown the ground beef and the shallots (around 5-6 minutes).
2. Add the garlic and spices and toss to mix well. Cook until meat will become brown and shallots will be soft and transparent. Add half of the enchilada sauce toss and cook for another 5 minutes.
3. Lightly toast the corn tortillas for 30-40 seconds on the toaster.
4. Distribute in each the remaining enchilada sauce and the ground beef mixture. Wrap and roll from one side to another to make enchiladas.
5. Sprinkle optionally a bit of grated cheddar cheese on top and place in the microwave for 1-2 minutes to melt the cheese and serve.

Per Serving

calories: 287 | fat: 8.9g | carbs: 30.8g | phosphorus: 146mg | potassium: 225mg
sodium: 202mg | protein: 26.3g

Italian Beef Meatballs

- 1½ pounds (680 g) ground beef chuck,
- 2 eggs, beaten
- ½ cup red onion, chopped
- ½ cup rolled oat flakes
- ½ teaspoon garlic salt
- 1 teaspoon dried oregano
- 3 tablespoons Parmesan cheese
- ½ teaspoon black pepper

1. Preheat your oven at 375ºF (190ºC).
2. Mix all the ingredients in a large bowl.
3. Shape into small balls (around 1 inch) and place on a Pyrex or baking sheet.
4. Bake for 15-17 minutes (or until they are fully cooked and slightly brown on the outside).
5. Remove from the oven and serve.

Per Serving

calories: 133 | fat: 5.3g | carbs: 5.8g | phosphorus: 167mg | potassium: 253mg
sodium: 63mg | protein: 14.5g

Rice and Beef Soup

Prep time: 15 minutes | Cook time: 40 minutes | Serves 6

- ½ pound (227 g) extra-lean ground beef
- ½ small sweet onion, chopped
- 1 teaspoon minced garlic
- 2 cups water
- 1 cup homemade low-sodium beef broth
- ½ cup long-grain white rice, uncooked
- 1 celery stalk, chopped
- ½ cup fresh green beans, cut into 1-inch pieces
- 1 teaspoon chopped fresh thyme
- Freshly ground black pepper, to taste

1. Place a large saucepan over medium-high heat and add the ground beef.
2. Sauté, stirring often, for about 6 minutes or until the beef is completely browned.
3. Drain off the excess fat and add the onion and garlic to the saucepan.
4. Sauté the vegetables for about 3 minutes or until they are softened.
5. Add the water, beef broth, rice, and celery.
6. Bring the soup to a boil, reduce the heat to low, and simmer for about 30 minutes or until the rice is tender.
7. Add the green beans and thyme and simmer for 3 minutes.
8. Remove the soup from the heat and season with pepper.

Per Serving

calories: 155 | fat: 6.9g | carbs: 13.9g | phosphorus: 75mg | potassium: 180mg
sodium: 134mg | protein: 8.8g

Beef and Veggie Stew

Prep time: 30 minutes | Cook time: 75 minutes | Serves 6

- ¼ cup all-purpose flour
- 1 teaspoon freshly ground black pepper, plus extra for seasoning
- Pinch cayenne pepper
- ½ pound (227 g) boneless beef chuck roast, trimmed of fat and cut into 1-inch chunks
- 2 tablespoons olive oil
- ½ sweet onion, chopped
- 2 teaspoons minced garlic
- 1 cup homemade beef stock
- 1 cup plus 2 tablespoons water
- 1 carrot, cut into ½-inch chunks
- 2 celery stalks, chopped with greens
- 1 teaspoon chopped fresh thyme
- 1 teaspoon cornstarch
- 2 tablespoons chopped fresh parsley

1. Preheat the oven to 350ºF (180ºC).
2. Put the flour, black pepper, and cayenne pepper in a large plastic freezer bag and toss to mix.

3. Add the beef chunks to the bag and toss to coat.
4. In a large ovenproof pot, heat the olive oil.
5. Sauté the beef chunks for about 5 minutes or until they are lightly browned. Remove the beef from the pot and set aside on a plate.
6. Add the onion and garlic to the pot and sauté for 3 minutes.
7. Stir in the beef stock and deglaze the pot, scraping up any bits on the bottom.
8. Add 1 cup water, the beef drippings on the plate, the carrot, celery, and thyme.
9. Cover the pot tightly with a lid or aluminum foil and place in the oven.
10. Bake the stew, stirring occasionally, for about 1 hour or until the meat is very tender.
11. Remove the stew from the oven.
12. In a small bowl, stir together the 2 tablespoons water and the cornstarch and then stir the mixture into the hot stew to thicken the sauce.
13. Season the stew with black pepper and serve topped with parsley.

Per Serving

calories: 164 | fat: 10.2g | carbs: 6.8g | phosphorus: 90mg | potassium: 201mg
sodium: 120mg | protein: 10.8g

Creamy Mustard Steak

Prep time: 10 minutes | Cook time: 8 minutes | Serves 4

- 2 tablespoons grainy mustard
- 1 tablespoon apple cider vinegar
- 1 tablespoon honey
- 1 teaspoon minced garlic
- 12 ounces (340 g) sirloin steak
- Pinch freshly ground black pepper

1. In a small bowl, stir together the mustard, vinegar, honey, and garlic.
2. Lightly season the steak with pepper.
3. Baste the steak generously with the mustard sauce on both sides, and let it stand for 15 minutes at room temperature.
4. Preheat the oven to broil, and set a rack in the top third of the oven.
5. Place a wire rack in a baking sheet, and arrange the steak on the rack.
6. Broil the steak, turning once and basting again, until the steak is browned and cooked to medium doneness, about 8 minutes total.
7. Serve hot.

Per Serving

calories: 137 | fat: 3.0g | carbs: 4.8g | phosphorus: 183mg | potassium: 307mg
sodium: 135mg | protein: 19.2g

Pork and Mushroom with Peanut Sauce

Prep time: 20 minutes | Cook time: 10 minutes | Serves 6

- ⅓ cup crunchy peanut butter
- ½ cup low-sodium chicken broth
- 2 tablespoons freshly squeezed lemon juice
- ⅛ teaspoon red pepper flakes
- 2 tablespoons olive oil
- 1 pound (454 g) pork tenderloin, cut
- into 1-inch slices
- ⅛ teaspoon cayenne pepper
- 1 onion, chopped
- 2 garlic cloves, minced
- 1 (8-ounce / 227-g) package sliced mushrooms
- ⅓ cup grated carrots

1. In a small bowl, stir together the peanut butter, chicken broth, lemon juice, and red pepper flakes and set aside.
2. Heat the olive oil in a large skillet over medium heat.
3. Sprinkle the tenderloin slices with the cayenne pepper and place in the skillet.
4. Cook the pork, turning once, until it registers 145ºF (63ºC) internal temperature. This should take 5 to 6 minutes in total.
5. Remove the pork from the skillet and set aside on a clean plate.
6. Add the onion, garlic, mushrooms, and carrot to the skillet. Sauté for 2 to 4 minutes or until tender-crisp.
7. Add the peanut sauce to the skillet and sauté for 1 minute. Then return the pork to the skillet and sauté for 1 to 2 minutes until heated through. Serve.

Per Serving

calories: 279 | fat: 15.8g | carbs: 7.9g | phosphorus: 318mg | potassium: 594mg
sodium: 124mg | protein: 25.8g

Pork, Pineapple, and Peach Kebabs

Prep time: 20 minutes | Cook time: 10 minutes | Serves 4

- 8 ounces (227 g) boneless pork loin chops, cubed
- 1 cup canned pineapple chunks, drained, reserving ¼ cup juice
- 2 peaches, peeled and cubed
- 4 scallions, white and green parts,
- cut into 2-inch pieces
- 2 tablespoons olive oil
- Juice of 1 lemon
- 2 tablespoons mustard
- 1 tablespoon cornstarch
- 2 teaspoons packed brown sugar

1. Prepare and preheat the grill to medium coals and set a grill 6 inches from the coals.
2. Thread the pork cubes, pineapple, peach cubes, and scallion pieces onto 4 (10-inch) metal skewers. Drizzle the kebabs with olive oil and set aside.

3. In a small saucepan, stir together the reserved pineapple juice, lemon juice, mustard, cornstarch, and brown sugar and bring to a simmer over medium heat. Simmer for 2 to 3 minutes or until the sauce boils and thickens. Remove from heat.
4. Place the kebabs on the grill. Grill for 8 to 10 minutes, turning frequently and brushing with the sauce until the pork registers at least 145ºF (63ºC) internal temperature. Use all of the sauce.
5. Remove the kebabs from the heat and let stand for 5 minutes before serving.
6. Ingredient Tip: Pork can be cooked to medium-well and still be considered food safe. Cook it to at least 145ºF (63ºC), measured with a meat thermometer, and let the pork stand for 5 minutes. This wait time will raise the temperature to 145ºF (63ºC) and maintain its juiciness.

Per Serving

calories: 274 | fat: 13.1g | carbs: 22.1g | phosphorus: 157mg | potassium: 470mg
sodium: 120mg | protein: 17.8g

Beef, Corn, and Black Bean Quesadillas

Prep time: 10 minutes | Cook time: 20 minutes | Serves 6

- ½ pound (227 g) 85-percent-lean ground beef
- 1 onion, chopped
- 1 cup frozen corn, thawed and drained
- ½ cup low-sodium or no-salt-added canned black beans, drained and
- rinsed
- 2 teaspoons chili powder
- ¼ teaspoon garlic powder
- 6 (6-inch) corn tortillas
- 1 cup shredded Colby-Jack cheese
- 6 tablespoons sour cream

1. In a medium saucepan over medium heat, sauté the ground beef and onion until the meat is browned and cooked through, 5 to 7 minutes. Remove the pan from the heat and drain off the excess fat.
2. Stir in the corn, beans, chili powder, and garlic powder into the meat mixture.
3. Place the tortillas on your work surface. Divide the beef mixture among half of the tortillas, spreading it out to about ½-inch from the edges. Top with the cheese and the remaining tortillas.
4. Place a large skillet over medium-high heat. Add the quesadillas one at a time. Cook for 2 to 3 minutes on each side, turning once, until the tortillas are crisp.
5. Repeat until all are cooked.
6. Cut each quesadilla into fourths with a sharp butcher knife and serve with the sour cream.

Per Serving

calories: 289 | fat: 14.9g | carbs: 32.8g | phosphorus: 275mg | potassium: 367mg
sodium: 317mg | protein: 17.8g

Authentic Salisbury Steak

Prep time: 15 minutes | Cook time: 25 minutes | Serves 4

- 12 ounces (340 g) lean ground beef
- 1 small sweet onion, finely chopped
- ½ red bell pepper, seeded and finely chopped
- 1 teaspoon minced garlic
- 1 egg, beaten
- ½ teaspoon chopped fresh thyme
- ¼ teaspoon freshly ground black pepper
- 1 teaspoon olive oil
- ½ cup sodium-free beef stock, divided
- 1 tablespoon cornstarch

1. In a medium bowl, mix together the beef, onion, bell pepper, garlic, egg, thyme, and pepper.
2. Form the meat mixture into 4 equal patties about ½ inch thick.
3. In a medium skillet over medium-high heat, heat the olive oil. Brown the patties on both sides, about 6 minutes total.
4. Add ¼ cup of stock to the skillet and simmer for 15 minutes, turning the patties once.
5. Remove the patties to a plate, cover, and set aside.
6. Whisk the cornstarch into the remaining ¼ cup of stock, and add the mixture to the skillet.
7. Simmer, whisking, until the sauce thickens to a gravy consistency.
8. Serve the patties topped with the sauce.

Per Serving

calories: 154 | fat: 6.8g | carbs: 1.9g | phosphorus: 194mg | potassium: 360mg
sodium: 118mg | protein: 19.8g

Brown Rice Stuffed Mini Beef Meatloaves

Prep time: 20 minutes | Cook time: 50 minutes | Makes 5 mini loaves

- Olive oil cooking spray
- 1½ cups water, plus 2 tablespoons
- 10 tablespoons uncooked brown rice
- 1¼ pounds (567 g) extra-lean ground beef
- 1 large egg yolk
- 3 tablespoons mustard, divided
- Pinch salt
- Pinch freshly ground black pepper
- ½ cup sour cream

1. Preheat the oven to 350ºF (180ºC). Spray a 6-cup muffin tin with cooking spray and set aside.
2. In a medium saucepan, combine the water and brown rice over medium heat. Bring to a boil, then reduce the heat, cover, and simmer for 25 to 30 minutes or until the rice is tender. Drain if necessary and set aside to cool for 20 minutes.

3. Meanwhile, in a medium bowl, combine the ground beef, egg yolk, 1 tablespoon of mustard, the salt, and pepper and mix well. Divide the beef mixture into 5 balls and press into the prepared cups against the sides and bottom, making a "crust," leaving a space for the filling.
4. In a small bowl, combine the remaining 2 tablespoons of mustard with the sour cream and mix them together. Add the sour cream mixture to the rice and mix them together. Spoon about ¼ cup of the rice mixture into the center of the beef cups. Put 2 tablespoons of water in the empty muffin cup.
5. Bake the meatloaves for 22 to 27 minutes or until a food thermometer inserted into the center reads 160°F (71°C) and the juices run clear. Let cool for 5 minutes, then carefully remove from the muffin tins and serve.

Per Serving (1 meatloaf)

calories: 345 | fat: 14.1g | carbs: 19.1g | phosphorus: 340mg | potassium: 463mg sodium: 211mg | protein: 33.8g

Beef and Rice Stuffed Peppers

Prep time: 15 minutes | Cook time: 45 minutes | Serves 4

- Olive oil, for the baking dish
- 4 red bell peppers, tops removed, seeded
- 8 ounces (227 g) lean ground beef
- ½ small sweet onion, finely chopped
- 1 celery stalk, finely chopped
- 1 teaspoon minced garlic
- ½ cup cooked white rice
- 1 teaspoon chopped fresh oregano
- ½ teaspoon chopped fresh thyme
- Freshly ground black pepper, to taste
- 2 tablespoons crumbled feta cheese

1. Preheat the oven to 350°F (180°C).
2. Lightly oil a baking dish, and place the peppers in, hollow-side up.
3. In a large skillet over medium-high heat, add the ground beef, and brown for about 10 minutes.
4. Stir in the onion, celery, and garlic, and sauté until the vegetables are softened, about 3 minutes.
5. Stir in the rice, oregano, and thyme.
6. Season the filling with pepper, and remove from the heat.
7. Spoon the filling into the 4 peppers, dividing it evenly, and sprinkle with the feta cheese.
8. Bake the peppers until tender and the filling is heated through, about 30 minutes.
9. Serve hot.

Per Serving

calories: 153 | fat: 4.9g | carbs: 10.9g | phosphorus: 175mg | potassium: 374mg sodium: 140mg | protein: 14.8g

CHAPTER 7

FISH AND SEAFOOD

Salmon and Asparagus Linguine

Prep time: 15 minutes | Cook time: 15 minutes | Serves 4

- ½ cup ricotta cheese
- ¼ cup heavy (whipping) cream
- Juice and zest of ½ lemon
- 1 tablespoon chopped fresh thyme
- ¼ teaspoon freshly ground black pepper
- 6 ounces (170 g) cooked or canned salmon, broken into chunks
- 1 cup (2-inch pieces) blanched asparagus spears
- 2 cups warm cooked linguine

1. In a medium saucepan, whisk together the ricotta cheese, cream, lemon juice, lemon zest, thyme, and pepper until well blended.
2. Place the saucepan over medium heat and cook, whisking frequently, until the sauce is hot and bubbly, about 10 minutes.
3. Stir in the salmon, asparagus, and linguine, and heat for 4 additional minutes.
4. Serve.

Per Serving

calories: 286 | fat: 12.8g | carbs: 24.7g | phosphorus: 234mg | potassium: 303mg
sodium: 64mg | protein: 16.8g

Crab and Spinach Soup

Prep time: 15 minutes | Cook time: 10 minutes | Serves 4

- 2 tablespoons extra-virgin olive oil
- 2 shallots, minced
- 8 ounces (227 g) fresh lump crab meat, picked over
- 4 cups low-sodium vegetable broth
- 2 cups roughly chopped baby spinach leaves
- ½ teaspoon Old Bay Seasoning
- ⅛ teaspoon freshly ground black pepper

1. In a medium saucepan, heat the olive oil over medium heat. Cook the shallots for about 3 minutes, stirring, until tender.
2. Add the crab meat and cook for 1 minute. Add the vegetable broth and bring to a simmer. Reduce the heat to low.
3. Add the spinach leaves, Old Bay Seasoning mix, and pepper. Simmer until the spinach is wilted and the soup is hot. Serve.

Per Serving

calories: 137 | fat: 6.9g | carbs: 5.9g | phosphorus: 158mg | potassium: 344mg
sodium: 400mg | protein: 11.9g

Baked Salmon with Greens

Prep time: 10 minutes | Cook time: 20 minutes | Serves 4

- 1 tablespoon olive oil, plus more for the baking dish
- 4 (2-ounce / 57-g) boneless skinless salmon fillets
- Freshly ground black pepper, to taste
- 1 cup (2-inch pieces) asparagus spears
- 1 cup quartered bok choy
- 2 tablespoons chopped fresh dill
- Juice and zest of 1 lemon

1. Preheat the oven to 375ºF (190ºC).
2. Lightly coat a baking dish with olive oil.
3. Lightly season the fish with pepper.
4. In the prepared baking dish, arrange the asparagus, bok choy, and dill, and top the vegetables with the fish fillets.
5. Sprinkle the lemon juice and lemon zest on the fish, and drizzle 1 tablespoon of olive oil over the salmon and vegetables.
6. Cover the dish with foil, and bake until the greens are tender and the fish flakes when pressed lightly, about 20 minutes.

Per Serving

calories: 135 | fat: 8.8g | carbs: 1.9g | phosphorus: 184mg | potassium: 297mg sodium: 35mg | protein: 11.9g

Sole Taco with Cabbage Coleslaw

Prep time: 15 minutes | Cook time: 10 minutes | Serves 4

- 2 tablespoons extra-virgin olive oil
- 2 shallots, minced
- 3 (6-ounce / 170-g) sole fillets, cut into strips
- 2 teaspoons chili powder
- 1 lime, zested and juiced
- 3 cups cabbage coleslaw mix with carrots

1. In a large skillet, heat the olive oil over medium heat.
2. Add the shallots and cook for 3 minutes, stirring, until softened.
3. Add the sole fillets and sprinkle with the chili powder. Cook for 3 to 5 minutes, stirring gently, until the fish flakes when tested with a fork. Remove the skillet from the heat.
4. Drizzle the lime zest and juice over the fish.
5. Serve with the coleslaw in tacos or over rice.

Per Serving

calories: 177 | fat: 8.9g | carbs: 13.9g | phosphorus: 266mg | potassium: 450mg sodium: 314mg | protein: 12.8g

Roasted Plums and Cod Fillets

Prep time: 10 minutes | Cook time: 20 minutes | Serves 4

- 6 red plums, halved and pitted
- 1½ pounds (680 g) cod fillets
- 3 tablespoons extra-virgin olive oil
- 2 tablespoons freshly squeezed lemon juice
- ½ teaspoon dried thyme leaves
- ⅛ teaspoon salt
- ⅛ teaspoon freshly ground black pepper
- ¾ cup plain whole-milk yogurt, for serving

1. Preheat the oven to 375ºF (190ºC). Line a baking sheet with parchment paper.
2. Arrange the plums, cut-side up, along with the fish on the prepared baking sheet. Drizzle with the olive oil and lemon juice and sprinkle with the thyme, salt, and pepper.
3. Roast for 15 to 20 minutes or until the fish flakes when tested with a fork and the plums are tender.
4. Serve with the yogurt.

Per Serving

calories: 231 | fat: 8.8g | carbs: 10.1g | phosphorus: 200mg | potassium: 436mg sodium: 153mg | protein: 26.9g

Scampi Linguine

Prep time: 15 minutes | Cook time: 15 minutes | Serves 4

- 4 ounces (113 g) uncooked linguine
- 1 teaspoon olive oil
- 2 teaspoons minced garlic
- 4 ounces (113 g) scampi, peeled, deveined, and chopped
- ½ cup dry white wine
- Juice of 1 lemon
- 1 tablespoon chopped fresh basil
- ½ cup heavy (whipping) cream
- Freshly ground black pepper, to taste

1. Cook the linguine according to the package instructions; drain and set aside.
2. In a large skillet over medium heat, heat the olive oil.
3. Sauté the garlic and scampi for about 6 minutes or until the scampi is opaque and just cooked through.
4. Add the wine, lemon juice, and basil, and cook for 5 minutes.
5. Stir in the cream and simmer for 2 minutes more.
6. Add the linguine to the skillet and toss to coat.
7. Divide the pasta onto 4 plates to serve.

Per Serving

calories: 220 | fat: 6.9g | carbs: 20.9g | phosphorus: 118mg | potassium: 154mg sodium: 41mg | protein: 11.8g

Honey Glazed Salmon

Prep time: 10 minutes | Cook time: 10 minutes | Serves 4

- 2 tablespoons honey
- 1 teaspoon lemon zest
- ½ teaspoon freshly ground black pepper
- 4 (3-ounce/ 85-g) salmon fillets
- 1 tablespoon olive oil
- ½ scallion, white and green parts, chopped

1. In a small bowl, stir together the honey, lemon zest, and pepper.
2. Wash the salmon and pat dry with paper towels.
3. Rub the honey mixture all over each fillet.
4. In a large skillet over medium heat, heat the olive oil.
5. Add the salmon fillets and cook the salmon for about 10 minutes, turning once, or until it is lightly browned and just cooked through.
6. Serve topped with chopped scallion.

Per Serving

calories: 238 | fat: 14.9g | carbs: 8.9g | phosphorus: 200mg | potassium: 370mg
sodium: 50mg | protein: 16.9g

Herbed Haddock

Prep time: 10 minutes | Cook time: 20 minutes | Serves 4

- ½ cup bread crumbs
- 3 tablespoons chopped fresh parsley
- 1 tablespoon lemon zest
- 1 teaspoon chopped fresh thyme
- ¼ teaspoon freshly ground black
- pepper
- 1 tablespoon melted unsalted butter
- 12 ounces (340 g) haddock fillets, deboned and skinned

1. Preheat the oven to 350ºF (180ºC).
2. In a small bowl, stir together the bread crumbs, parsley, lemon zest, thyme, and pepper until well combined.
3. Add the melted butter and toss until the mixture resembles coarse crumbs.
4. Place the haddock on a baking sheet and spoon the bread crumb mixture on top, pressing down firmly.
5. Bake the haddock in the oven for about 20 minutes or until the fish is just cooked through and flakes off in chunks when pressed.

Per Serving

calories: 144 | fat: 3.8g | carbs: 9.8g | phosphorus: 215mg | potassium: 284mg
sodium: 280mg | protein: 15.8g

Shrimp and Snow Peas Stir-Fry

Prep time: 20 minutes | Cook time: 12 minutes | Serves 4

- 2 tablespoons extra-virgin olive oil
- 1 tablespoon minced peeled fresh ginger
- 2 cups snow peas
- 1½ cups frozen baby peas
- 3 tablespoons water
- 1 pound (454 g) medium shrimp, shelled and deveined
- 2 tablespoons low-sodium soy sauce
- ⅛ teaspoon freshly ground black pepper

1. In a large wok or skillet, heat the olive oil over medium heat.
2. Add the ginger and stir-fry for 1 to 2 minutes, until the ginger is fragrant.
3. Add the snow peas and stir-fry for 2 to 3 minutes, until they are tender-crisp.
4. Add the baby peas and the water and stir. Cover the wok and steam for 2 to 3 minutes or until the vegetables are tender.
5. Stir in the shrimp and stir-fry for 3 to 4 minutes, or until the shrimp have curled and turned pink.
6. Add the soy sauce and pepper; stir and serve.

Per Serving

calories: 236 | fat: 6.9g | carbs: 11.8g | phosphorus: 348mg | potassium: 500mg sodium: 468mg | protein: 31.8g

Simple Scallion Sole

Prep time: 20 minutes | Cook time: 10 minutes | Serves 4

- ¼ cup all-purpose flour
- ¼ teaspoon freshly ground black pepper
- 12 ounces (340 g) sole fillets, deboned and skinned
- 2 tablespoons olive oil
- 1 scallion, both green and white parts, chopped
- Lemon wedges, for garnish

1. In a large plastic freezer bag, shake together the flour and pepper to combine.
2. Add the fish fillets to the flour and shake to coat.
3. In a large skillet over medium-high heat, heat the olive oil.
4. When the oil is hot, add the fish fillets and fry for about 10 minutes, turning once, or until they are golden and cooked through.
5. Remove the fish from the oil onto paper towels to drain.
6. Serve topped with chopped scallions and a squeeze of lemon.

Per Serving

calories: 150 | fat: 7.9g | carbs: 5.9g | phosphorus: 222mg | potassium: 146mg sodium: 240mg | protein: 10.9g

Grilled Shrimp with Lime-Cucumber Salsa

Prep time: 15 minutes | Cook time: 10 minutes | Serves 4

- 2 tablespoons olive oil
- 6 ounces (170 g) large shrimp (16 to 20 count), peeled and deveined, tails left on
- 1 teaspoon minced garlic
- ½ cup chopped English cucumber
- ½ cup chopped mango
- Zest of 1 lime
- Juice of 1 lime
- Freshly ground black pepper, to taste
- Lime wedges for garnish

1. Soak 4 wooden skewers in water for 30 minutes.
2. Preheat the barbecue to medium-high heat.
3. In a large bowl, toss together the olive oil, shrimp, and garlic.
4. Thread the shrimp onto the skewers, about 4 shrimp per skewer.
5. In a small bowl, stir together the cucumber, mango, lime zest, and lime juice, and season the salsa lightly with pepper. Set aside.
6. Grill the shrimp for about 10 minutes, turning once or until the shrimp is opaque and cooked through.
7. Season the shrimp lightly with pepper.
8. Serve the shrimp on the cucumber salsa with lime wedges on the side.

Per Serving

calories: 119 | fat: 7.9g | carbs: 3.9g | phosphorus: 90mg | potassium: 128mg sodium: 59mg | protein: 8.9g

Herbed Calamari

Prep time: 10 minutes | Cook time: 3 minutes | Serves 4

- 2 tablespoons olive oil
- 2 tablespoons freshly squeezed lemon juice
- 1 tablespoon chopped fresh parsley
- 1 tablespoon chopped fresh oregano
- 2 teaspoons minced garlic
- Pinch sea salt
- Pinch freshly ground black pepper
- ½ pound (227 g) cleaned calamari
- Lemon wedges, for garnish

1. In large bowl, stir together the olive oil, lemon juice, parsley, oregano, garlic, salt, and pepper.
2. Add the calamari to the bowl and stir to coat.
3. Cover the bowl and refrigerate the calamari for 1 hour to marinate.
4. Preheat the barbecue to medium-high.
5. Grill the calamari, turning once, until firm and opaque, about 3 minutes total.
6. Serve with lemon wedges.

Per Serving

calories: 80 | fat: 6.8g | carbs: 1.8g | phosphorus: 126mg | potassium: 159mg sodium: 66mg | protein: 2.9g

Marinated Shrimp and Veggies with Penne

Prep time: 15 minutes | Cook time: 10 minutes | Serves 10

- 12 ounces (340 g) three-colored penne pasta
- ½ pound (227 g) cooked shrimp
- ½ red bell pepper, diced
- ½ cup red onion, chopped
- 3 stalks celery
- 12 baby carrots, cut into thick slices
- 1 cup cauliflower, cut into small round pieces
- ¼ cup honey
- ¼ cup balsamic vinegar
- ½ teaspoon black pepper
- ½ teaspoon garlic powder
- 1 tablespoon French mustard
- ¾ cup olive oil

1. Cook pasta for around 10 minutes (or according to packaged instructions).
2. While pasta is boiling, cut all your veggies and place into a large mixing bowl. Add the cooked shrimp.
3. In a mixing bowl, add the honey, vinegar, black pepper, garlic powder, and mustard.
4. While you whisk, slowly incorporate the oil and stir well.
5. Add in the drained pasta with the veggies and shrimp and gently combine everything together.
6. Pour the liquid marinade over the pasta and veggies and toss to coat everything evenly.
7. Refrigerate for 3 to 5 hours prior to serving.
8. Serve chilled.

Per Serving

calories: 255 | fat: 16.9g | carbs: 40.9g | phosphorus: 86mg | potassium: 132mg sodium: 242mg | protein: 6.6g

Cod with Cucumber Salsa

Prep time: 20 minutes | Cook time: 10 minutes | Serves 4

For the Cucumber Salsa:

- ½ English cucumber, chopped
- 2 tablespoons chopped fresh dill
- Juice of 1 lime
- Zest of 1 lime
- ¼ cup boiled and minced red bell pepper
- ½ teaspoon granulated sugar

For the Fish:

- 12 ounces (340 g) cod fillets, deboned and cut into 4 servings
- Juice of 1 lemon
- ½ teaspoon freshly ground black pepper
- 1 teaspoon olive oil

To Make the Cucumber Salsa

1. In a small bowl, mix together the cucumber, dill, lime juice, lime zest, red pepper, and sugar; set aside.

To Make the Fish

1. Preheat the oven to 350ºF (180ºC).
2. Place the fish on a pie plate and squeeze the lemon juice evenly over the fillets.
3. Sprinkle with pepper and drizzle the olive oil evenly over the fillets.
4. Bake the fish for about 6 minutes or until it flakes easily with a fork.
5. Transfer the fish to 4 plates and serve topped with cucumber salsa.

Per Serving

calories: 109 | fat: 1.9g | carbs: 2.9g | phosphorus: 118mg | potassium: 274mg
sodium: 66mg | protein: 19.8g

Golden Crab Cakes with Cucumber Salsa

Prep time: 20 minutes | Cook time: 20 minutes | Serves 4

For the Salsa:

- ½ English cucumber, diced
- 1 lime, chopped
- ½ cup boiled and chopped red bell pepper
- 1 teaspoon chopped fresh cilantro
- Freshly ground black pepper, to taste

For the Crab Cakes:

- 8 ounces (227 g) queen crab meat
- ¼ cup bread crumbs
- 1 small egg
- ¼ cup boiled and chopped red bell pepper
- 1 scallion, both green and white parts, minced
- 1 tablespoon chopped fresh parsley
- Splash hot sauce
- Olive oil spray, for the pan

To Make the Salsa

1. In a small bowl, stir together the cucumber, lime, red pepper, and cilantro.
2. Season with pepper; set aside.

To Make the Crab Cakes

1. In a medium bowl, mix together the crab, bread crumbs, egg, red pepper, scallion, parsley, and hot sauce until it holds together. Add more bread crumbs, if necessary.
2. Form the crab mixture into 4 patties and place them on a plate.
3. Refrigerate the crab cakes for 1 hour to firm them.
4. Spray a large skillet generously with olive oil spray and place it over medium-high heat.
5. Cook the crab cakes in batches, turning, for about 5 minutes per side or until golden brown.
6. Serve the crab cakes with the salsa.

Per Serving

calories: 116 | fat: 1.9g | carbs: 6.9g | phosphorus: 108mg | potassium: 199mg
sodium: 420mg | protein: 15.8g

CHAPTER 8

SNACKS

Kettle Corn

Prep time: 1 minute | Cook time: 5 minutes | Serves 8

- 3 tablespoons olive oil
- 1 cup popcorn kernels
- ½ cup brown sugar
- Pinch cayenne pepper

1. Place a large pot with lid over medium heat and add the olive oil with a few popcorn kernels.
2. Shake the pot lightly until the popcorn kernels pop. Add the rest of the kernels and sugar to the pot.
3. Pop the kernels with the lid on the pot, shaking constantly, until they are all popped.
4. Remove the pot from the heat and transfer the popcorn to a large bowl.
5. Toss the popcorn with the cayenne pepper and serve.

Per Serving

calories: 187 | fat: 5.9g | carbs: 29.8g | phosphorus: 84mg | potassium: 89mg
sodium: 4mg | protein: 2.9g

Tortilla Chips

Prep time: 15 minutes | Cook time: 10 minutes | Serves 6

- 2 teaspoons granulated sugar
- ½ teaspoon ground cinnamon
- Pinch ground nutmeg
- 3 (6-inch) flour tortillas
- Cooking spray, for coating the tortillas

1. Preheat the oven to 350ºF (180ºC).
2. Line a baking sheet with parchment paper.
3. In a small bowl, stir together the sugar, cinnamon, and nutmeg.
4. Lay the tortillas on a clean work surface and spray both sides of each lightly with cooking spray.
5. Sprinkle the cinnamon sugar evenly over both sides of each tortilla.
6. Cut the tortillas into 16 wedges each and place them on the baking sheet.
7. Bake the tortilla wedges, turning once, for about 10 minutes or until crisp.
8. Cool the chips and store in a sealed container at room temperature for up to 1 week.

Per Serving

calories: 50 | fat: 0.9g | carbs: 8.9g | phosphorus: 28mg | potassium: 23mg
sodium: 102mg | protein: 0.8g

Collard Chips

Prep time: 5 minutes | Cook time: 20 minutes | Serves 4

- 1 bunch collard greens
- 1 teaspoon extra-virgin olive oil
- Juice of ½ lemon
- ½ teaspoon garlic powder
- ¼ teaspoon freshly ground black pepper

1. Preheat the oven to 350ºF (180ºC). Line a baking sheet with parchment paper.
2. Cut the collards into 2-by-2-inch squares and pat dry with paper towels. In a large bowl, toss the greens with the olive oil, lemon juice, garlic powder, and pepper. Use your hands to mix well, massaging the dressing into the greens until evenly coated.
3. Arrange the collards in a single layer on the baking sheet, and cook for 8 minutes. Flip the pieces and cook for an additional 8 minutes, until crisp. Remove from the oven, let cool, and store in an airtight container in a cool location for up to three days.

Per Serving

calories: 23 | fat: 0.9g | carbs: 2.9g | phosphorus: 5mg | potassium: 71mg
sodium: 7mg | protein: 0.9g

Chicken and Pepper Crostini

Prep time: 10 minutes | Cook time: 5 minutes | Serves 4

- 2 tablespoons olive oil
- ½ teaspoon minced garlic
- 4 slices French bread
- 1 roasted red bell pepper, chopped
- 4 ounces (113 g) cooked chicken breast, shredded
- ½ cup chopped fresh basil

1. Preheat the oven to 400ºF (205ºC).
2. Line a baking sheet with aluminum foil.
3. In a small bowl, mix together the olive oil and garlic.
4. Brush both sides of each piece of bread with the olive oil mixture.
5. Place the bread on the baking sheet and toast in the oven, turning once, for about 5 minutes or until both sides are golden and crisp.
6. In a medium bowl, stir together the red pepper, chicken, and basil.
7. Top each toasted bread slice with the red pepper mixture and serve.

Per Serving

calories: 183 | fat: 7.9g | carbs: 18.8g | phosphorus: 86mg | potassium: 151mg
sodium: 174mg | protein: 8.9g

Apple Chips

Prep time: 5 minutes | Cook time: 2 to 3 hours | Serves 4

- 4 apples
- 1 teaspoon ground cinnamon

1. Preheat the oven to 200ºF (93ºC). Line a baking sheet with parchment paper.
2. Core the apples and cut into ⅛-inch slices.
3. In a medium bowl, toss the apple slices with the cinnamon. Spread the apples in a single layer on the prepared baking sheet.
4. Cook for 2 to 3 hours, until the apples are dry. They will still be soft while hot, but will crisp once completely cooled. Store in an airtight container for up to four days.

Per Serving

calories: 95 | fat: 0g | carbs: 25.8g | phosphorus: 0mg | potassium: 197mg
sodium: 1mg | protein: 1.1g

Roasted Turnips, Rutabaga, and Parsnips

Prep time: 10 minutes | Cook time: 25 minutes | Serves 6

- 1 cup chopped turnips
- 1 cup chopped rutabaga
- 1 cup chopped parsnips
- 1 tablespoon extra-virgin olive oil
- 1 teaspoon fresh chopped rosemary
- Freshly ground black pepper, to taste

1. Preheat the oven to 400ºF (205ºC).
2. In a large bowl, toss the turnips, rutabaga, and parsnips with the olive oil and rosemary. Arrange in a single layer on a baking sheet, and season with pepper.
3. Bake until the vegetables are tender and browned, 20 to 25 minutes, stirring once.

Per Serving

calories: 50 | fat: 1.9g | carbs: 6.9g | phosphorus: 34mg | potassium: 204mg
sodium: 21mg | protein: 0.9g

Syrian Baba Ghanoush

Prep time: 20 minutes | Cook time: 30 minutes | Serves 6

- 1 medium eggplant, halved and scored with a crosshatch pattern on the cut sides
- 1 tablespoon olive oil, plus extra for brushing
- 1 large sweet onion, peeled and diced
- 2 garlic cloves, halved
- 1 teaspoon ground cumin
- 1 teaspoon ground coriander
- 1 tablespoon lemon juice
- Freshly ground black pepper, to taste

1. Preheat the oven to 400°F (205°C).
2. Line 2 baking sheets with parchment paper.
3. Brush the eggplant halves with olive oil and place them, cut-side down, on 1 baking sheet.
4. In a small bowl, mix together the onion, garlic, 1 tablespoon olive oil, cumin, and coriander.
5. Spread the seasoned onions on the other baking sheet.
6. Place both baking sheets in the oven and roast the onions for about 20 minutes and the eggplant for 30 minutes, or until softened and browned.
7. Remove the vegetables from the oven and scrape the eggplant flesh into a bowl.
8. Transfer the onions and garlic to a cutting board and chop coarsely; add to the eggplant.
9. Stir in the lemon juice and pepper.
10. Serve warm or chilled.

Per Serving

calories: 44 | fat: 1.9g | carbs: 5.9g | phosphorus: 22mg | potassium: 194mg
sodium: 2mg | protein: 0.9g

Collard Salad Rolls

Prep time: 20 minutes | Cook time: 0 minutes | Serves 4

For the Dipping Sauce:
- ¼ cup peanut butter
- 2 tablespoons honey
- Juice of 1 lime
- ¼ teaspoon red chili flakes

For the Salad Rolls:
- 4 ounces (113 g) extra-firm tofu
- 1 bunch collard greens
- 1 cup thinly sliced purple cabbage
- 1 cup bean sprouts
- 2 carrots, cut into matchsticks
- ½ cup cilantro leaves and stems

To Make the Dipping Sauce

1. In a blender, combine the peanut butter, honey, lime juice, and chili flakes, and process until smooth. Add 1 to 2 tablespoons of water as desired for consistency.

To Make the Salad Rolls

1. Using paper towels, press the excess moisture from the tofu. Cut into ½-inch-thick matchsticks.
2. Remove any tough stems from the collard greens and set aside.
3. Arrange all of the ingredients within reach. Cup one collard green leaf in your hand, and add a couple pieces of the tofu and a small amount each of the cabbage, bean sprouts, and carrots. Top with a couple cilantro sprigs, and roll into a cylinder. Place each roll, seam-side down, on a serving platter while you assemble the rest of the rolls. Serve with the dipping sauce.

Per Serving

calories: 172 | fat: 8.8g | carbs: 19.8g | phosphorus: 57mg | potassium: 283mg sodium: 41mg | protein: 7.8g

Kale Chips

Prep time: 20 minutes | Cook time: 25 minutes | Serves 6

- 2 cups kale
- 2 teaspoons olive oil
- ¼ teaspoon chili powder
- Pinch cayenne pepper

1. Preheat the oven to 300ºF (150ºC).
2. Line 2 baking sheets with parchment paper; set aside.
3. Remove the stems from the kale and tear the leaves into 2-inch pieces.
4. Wash the kale and dry it completely.
5. Transfer the kale to a large bowl and drizzle with olive oil.
6. Use your hands to toss the kale with the oil, taking care to coat each leaf evenly.

7. Season the kale with chili powder and cayenne pepper and toss to combine thoroughly.
8. Spread the seasoned kale in a single layer on each baking sheet. Do not overlap the leaves.
9. Bake the kale, rotating the pans once, for 20 to 25 minutes or until it is crisp and dry.
10. Remove the trays from the oven and allow the chips to cool on the trays for 5 minutes.
11. Serve immediately.

Per Serving

calories: 23 | fat: 1.9g | carbs: 1.9g | phosphorus: 20mg | potassium: 110mg sodium: 12mg | protein: 0.9g

Mint Carrot Rroast

Prep time: 5 minutes | Cook time: 20 minutes | Serves 6

- 1 pound (454 g) carrots, trimmed
- 1 tablespoon extra-virgin olive oil
- Freshly ground black pepper, to taste
- ¼ cup thinly sliced mint

1. Preheat the oven to 425ºF (220ºC).
2. Arrange the carrots in a single layer on a rimmed baking sheet. Drizzle with the olive oil, and shake the carrots on the sheet to coat. Season with pepper.
3. Roast for 20 minutes, or until tender and browned, stirring twice while cooking. Sprinkle with the mint and serve.

Per Serving

calories: 50 | fat: 1.9g | carbs: 6.8g | phosphorus: 25mg | potassium: 241mg sodium: 50mg | protein: 0.9g

CHAPTER
9

DESSERTS

Tart Apple Pie

Prep time: 10 minutes | Cook time: 35 minutes | Serves 8

- 4 large tart apples, peeled, seeded and sliced
- ½ cup white all-purpose flour
- ⅓ cup margarine
- 1 cup sugar
- ¾ cup rolled oat flakes
- ½ teaspoon ground nutmeg

1. Preheat the oven to 375ºF (190ºC).
2. Place the apples over a lightly greased square pan (around 7 inches).
3. Mix the rest of the ingredients in a medium bowl with and spread the batter over the apples.
4. Bake for 30 to 35 minutes or until the top crust has gotten golden brown.
5. Serve hot.

Per Serving

calories: 262 | fat: 8.0g | carbs: 47.2g | phosphorus: 35mg | potassium: 124mg
sodium: 81mg | protein: 1.5g

Vanilla Cookies

Prep time: 10 minutes | Cook time: 12 minutes | Serves 12

- ¾ cup all-purpose flour
- ½ cup oatmeal
- ½ cup whey protein powder
- ¾ cups brown sugar
- 1 egg
- 1 teaspoon vanilla extract
- 1 teaspoon baking soda
- 3 tablespoons margarine

1. Preheat your oven at 325ºF (163ºC)
2. Beat with the mixer the butter and the brown sugar.
3. Add the egg and the vanilla extract
4. Combine all the other ingredients until smooth (the mixture will be a tad drier than most cookie doughs).
5. Roll the batter with your hands into 1"balls.
6. Lightly grease a baking sheet and the cookie balls.
7. Bake for 10 to 12 minutes.

Per Serving

calories: 293 | fat: 1.5g | carbs: 29.1g | phosphorus: 630mg | potassium: 291mg
sodium: 173mg | protein: 35.1g

Super Lemon Mousse

Prep time: 35 minutes | Cook time: 5 minutes | Serves 6

- 4 eggs, separated
- ½ cup sugar
- ¼ cup freshly squeezed lemon juice
- 1 tablespoon freshly grated lemon
- zest
- 1 teaspoon vanilla extract
- ½ cup heavy cream, whipped to stiff peaks

1. In a large bowl, beat the egg yolks until very thick and pale yellow.
2. Fold in the sugar by tablespoons, beating well after each addition, and scraping down the sides of the bowl.
3. Beat in the lemon juice and lemon zest.
4. Heat a large saucepan with about 2 inches of water to a boil.
5. Reduce the heat to low so the water is simmering. Place the bowl with the egg yolk mixture into the water.
6. Whisk the egg mixture until it thickens and coats the back of a spoon, about 5 minutes. Remove the bowl from the heat, and cool to room temperature.
7. Fold the whipped cream gently into the egg yolk mixture to lighten it, keeping as much volume as possible.
8. In another large bowl, beat the egg whites until they form stiff peaks.
9. Fold the egg whites into the lemon mousse carefully.
10. Spoon the lemon mousse into individual bowls and serve.

Per Serving

calories: 184 | fat: 10.9g | carbs: 17.9g | phosphorus: 75mg | potassium: 73mg sodium: 53mg | protein: 4.9g

Chocolate Pie Shell

Prep time: 5 minutes | Cook time: 30 minutes | Serves 6

- 3 cups cocoa rice Krispies, crushed
- ½ stick unsalted butter, melted

1. Place crushed cocoa Krispies in a bowl with the melted butter. Mix well with a spatula.
2. Spray a pie pan with some low-calorie cooking spray
3. Press the mixture into the pan and even out with a spatula.
4. Let sit and chill for at least 30 minutes in the fridge prior filling it with chocolate or vanilla pudding.

Per Serving

calories: 113 | fat: 7.8g | carbs: 11.6g | phosphorus: 18mg | potassium: 17mg sodium: 123mg | protein: 0.9g

Poached Pears with Apple Juice

Prep time: 15 minutes | Cook time: 30 minutes | Serves 4

- 4 cups water
- 2 cups apple juice
- 1 cup sugar
- 4 pears, peeled with the stem left on
- 1 vanilla bean, split and seeded

1. In a large saucepan over medium heat, add the water, apple juice, and sugar. Stir the mixture until the sugar is completely dissolved, then simmer for 5 minutes.
2. Add the pears and vanilla bean and seeds to the simmering liquid, and cover the saucepan.
3. Simmer the pears, turning several times, until the pears are very tender, about 20 minutes.
4. Carefully remove the pears from the liquid with a slotted spoon, and arrange on a plate. Serve warm or cooled.

Per Serving

calories: 147 | fat: 0g | carbs: 38.9g | phosphorus: 17mg | potassium: 196mg sodium: 2mg | protein: 0.9g

Pumpkin Pudding

Prep time: 10 minutes | Cook time: 8 to 10 minutes | Serves 4

- 3 ounces (85 g) instant vanilla pudding mix powder
- 1 cup almond milk
- ½ cup pumpkin puree
- 1 teaspoon pumpkin spice mix
- 1 scoop vanilla flavored protein powder

1. In a saucepan, mix the pudding mix and the almond milk.
2. Bring to a boil and reduce the heat as soon as the pudding has started to thicken.
3. Take off the heat and mix in the pumpkin puree, the pumpkin spice, and the protein powder. Stir well.
4. Transfer into a big glass bowl, let chill and cover with plastic wrap. Refrigerate for at least 5 hours prior to serving.

Per Serving

calories: 120 | fat: 0.8g | carbs: 22.8g | phosphorus: 164.6mg | potassium: 84mg sodium: 371mg | protein: 5.5g

Strawberry Sorbet

Prep time: 10 minutes | Cook time: 1 minutes | Serves 3 to 4

- ¼ cup white sugar
- 1 cup frozen or fresh, sliced strawberries
- 1 tablespoon lime juice
- ¼ cup water
- 1¼ cup crushed ice
- A few mint leaves

1. Pulse and crush the ice in a heavy-duty blender.
2. Add the remaining ingredients and raise the speed to crush until no lumps of ice are left.
3. Optionally add a few mint leaves for garnishing.

Per Serving

calories: 93 | fat: 0.1g | carbs: 32.0g | phosphorus: 10mg | potassium: 113mg
sodium: 2mg | protein: 0.3g

Lush Berry Galette

Prep time: 20 minutes | Cook time: 30 minutes | Serves 8

- 2 cups fresh blueberries
- 1 cup fresh raspberries
- ½ cup sugar
- 1 tablespoon cornstarch
- ¼ teaspoon ground nutmeg
- 1 (9-inch) prepared, flat, unbaked piecrust
- 1 egg, beaten

1. Preheat the oven to 400ºF (205ºC).
2. Line a baking sheet with parchment paper.
3. In a large bowl, add the blueberries, raspberries, sugar, cornstarch, and nutmeg and toss gently to mix together.
4. Lay the piecrust on the parchment paper in the prepared pan, and pour the berry mixture into the center.
5. Spread out the berries, leaving about 1½ inches of bare crust around the edges.
6. Brush the bare crust with the egg. Fold the edges of the crust back over the filling, pressing lightly so the overlapping pastry folds stick together.
7. Bake the galette until the crust is golden and crisp and the berries are bubbling, about 30 minutes.
8. Serve.

Per Serving

calories: 195 | fat: 4.8g | carbs: 44.9g | phosphorus: 18mg | potassium: 143mg
sodium: 55mg | protein: 3.9g

Creamsicle Lemon Cheesecake

Prep time: 20 minutes | Cook time: 0 minutes | Serves 8

- 1 envelope powdered gelatin
- ¼ cup cold water
- 14 ounces (397 g) plain cream cheese, at room temperature
- 3 tablespoons honey
- Juice and zest of ½ lemon
- 1 teaspoon vanilla extract
- 1 cup heavy cream, whipped to stiff peaks

1. Line the bottom of a springform pan with parchment paper.
2. In a small bowl, sprinkle the gelatin over the cold water and let it stand for 10 minutes.
3. In a large bowl, beat together the cream cheese, honey, lemon juice, lemon zest, and vanilla until smooth.
4. Beat the gelatin into the cream cheese mixture until well blended.
5. Gently fold the whipped cream into the cream cheese mixture, keeping as much volume as possible.
6. Transfer the cheesecake mixture to the springform pan, and chill in the refrigerator until firm, about 3 hours.
7. Run a knife around the edges of the pan and remove the ring.
8. Slice and serve.

Per Serving

calories: 299 | fat: 27.8g | carbs: 9.9g | phosphorus: 71mg | potassium: 104mg sodium: 170mg | protein: 3.9g

Pineapple and Mango Granita

Prep time: 5 minutes | Cook time: 0 minutes | Serves 4

- 1 cup fresh or frozen pineapple chunks
- ½ cup fresh or frozen mango chunks
- 2 cups lemon juice
- Juice of 1 lime
- Fresh mint, for garnish

1. In a blender, combine the pineapple, mango, lemon juice, and lime juice. Process until smooth, and transfer to a freezer-safe dish. Freeze for 2 hours.
2. Use a fork to break the mixture apart into smaller granular pieces. Serve garnished with pieces of torn mint leaves.

Per Serving

calories: 104 | fat: 0g | carbs: 25.8g | phosphorus: 12mg | potassium: 144mg sodium: 2mg | protein: 0.9g

Fast and Easy Grapefruit Sorbet

Prep time: 10 minutes | Cook time: 5 minutes | Serves 6

For the Thyme Simple Syrup:
- ½ cup sugar
- ¼ cup water
- 1 fresh thyme sprig

For the Sorbet:
- Juice of 6 pink grapefruit
- ¼ cup thyme simple syrup

To Make the Thyme Simple Syrup
1. In a small saucepan, combine the sugar, water, and thyme. Bring to a boil, turn off the heat, and refrigerate, thyme sprig included, until cold. Strain the thyme sprig from the syrup.

To Make the Sorbet
1. In a blender, combine the grapefruit juice and ¼ cup of simple syrup, and process.
2. Transfer to an airtight container and freeze for 3 to 4 hours, until firm. Serve.

Per Serving

calories: 108 | fat: 0g | carbs: 25.9g | phosphorus: 28mg | potassium: 317mg
sodium: 1mg | protein: 0.9g

Chocolate Fudge

Prep time: 10 minutes | Cook time: 10 minutes | Serves 12

- ⅔ cup half and half cream
- 1 cup white granulated sugar
- 1 cups semi-sweet chocolate chip
- cookies
- 1 cup mini marshmallows
- 1 teaspoon vanilla extract

1. Grease with cooking spray a square pie pan (around 9 inches).
2. Mix the half-and-half cream with the sugar in a medium saucepan. Bring to a boil and adjust to medium heat.
3. Take off the heat and add the chocolate chips, the marshmallows, and the vanilla extract. Stir well with a spatula until everything will be melted.
4. Quickly transfer the mixture into the pie pan. Let cool for at least 10 minutes and cut into square pieces, around 3x2" each. This will make 18-20 pieces.

Per Serving

calories: 52 | fat: 21.3g | carbs: 17.6g | phosphorus: 39mg | potassium: 101mg
sodium: 153mg | protein: 3.2g

Conclusion

Getting used to the renal diet takes a little time, a little patience, and just the right dose of perseverance.

Changing what you eat is never easy, regardless of what the purpose behind the change may be — and the renal diet is no exception from the rule.

The good news about this diet is that it does not require a superhuman effort on your side. Just a little bit of attention to detail and devotion to sticking to a series of basic health rules. Everything else will come naturally: the choices you make when you go into a supermarket, how you avoid take-out and sodas, how you start cooking your own meals, and, ultimately, how you embrace the renal diet as part of your life, rather than just a short-term solution.

Our hope is that the book at hand has helped you gain a deeper understanding of how our kidneys function and why diet is such an important element in managing kidney disease.

But more than anything, what we hope is that you have learned that the renal diet is not something to be afraid of — but something to look forward to in hope.

So? What are you waiting for? Open up your renal diet recipe book and dive right into this new, healthy life you choose for yourself!

You will never regret making this change!

References

Davita. (n.d.-a). Stages of Chronic Kidney Disease. https://www.davita.com/education/kidney-disease/stages

National Kidney Foundation. (n.d.). How Your Kidneys Work. https://www.kidney.org/kidneydisease/howkidneyswrk

NHS. (2019). Chronic kidney disease - Symptoms. https://www.nhs.uk/conditions/kidney-disease/symptoms/

Appendix 1: 4-week Meal Plan

Week 1	Breakfast	Lunch	Dinner	Snacks/Desserts
1	Bell Pepper Egg Muffins	Baked Salmon with Greens	Beef Hamburgers	Apple Chips
2	Almond and Rice Cereal	Thai Chicken and Cabbage Salad	Tunisian Chicken Thighs with Rice	Lush Berry Galette
3	Summer Omelet	Cod with Cucumber Salsa	Simple Scallion Sole	Collard Salad Rolls
4	Bell Pepper Egg Muffins	Shrimp and Snow Peas Stir-Fry	Crispy Chicken	Poached Pears with Apple Juice
5	Turmeric and Squash Omelet	Pasta Fasul	Honey Glazed Salmon	Syrian Baba Ghanoush
6	Golden Blueberry Scones	Alfredo Lasagna Spinach Rolls	Curried Turkey and Cauliflower	Chocolate Fudge
7	Bread and Rhubarb Pudding	Beef and Veggie Stew	Golden Crab Cakes with Cucumber Salsa	Kale Chips

Week 2	Breakfast	Lunch	Dinner	Snacks/Desserts
1	Breakfast Egg-In-A-Hole	Slow Cooked Kidney Bean Chili	Chicken and Carrot Patties	Chocolate Pie Shell
2	Golden Blueberry Scones	Red Coleslaw	Marinated Onion Chicken	Chicken and Pepper Crostini
3	Cucumber and Watercress Pita Pockets	Sole Taco with Cabbage Coleslaw	Herbed Calamari	Fast and Easy Grapefruit Sorbet

4	Bell Pepper Egg Muffins	Beef, Corn, and Black Bean Quesadillas	Pork and Mushroom with Peanut Sauce	Tortilla Chips
5	Turmeric and Squash Omelet	Cauliflower and Green Bean Biriyani	Stir-Fried Tofu and Broccoli	Creamsicle Lemon Cheesecake
6	Easy Tacos	Vietnamese Turkey and Cabbage Pho	Moroccan Chicken Stew	Pumpkin Pudding
7	Cranberry Almond Oats	Bulgur and Bean Stuffed Delicata Squash	Cabbage Quiche	Tart Apple Pie

Week 3	Breakfast	Lunch	Dinner	Snacks/Desserts
1	Bread and Rhubarb Pudding	Italian Turkey and Mushroom Kebabs	Asparagus and Turkey Risotto	Strawberry Sorbet
2	Simple Pancake	Cranberry and Bulgur Stuffed Spaghetti Squash	Creamy Mustard Steak	Mint Carrot Rroast
3	Golden Blueberry Scones	Chicken and Vegetable Casserole	Roasted Eggplan and Zucchini Barley Bowl	Vanilla Cookies
4	Turmeric and Squash Omelet	Arugula and Walnut Pesto Pasta	Roasted Summer Squash Sandwiches	Kettle Corn
5	Almond and Rice Cereal	Scampi Linguine	Italian Beef Meatballs	Chocolate Fudge
6	Bell Pepper Egg Muffins	Roasted Plums and Cod Fillets	Spinach and Falafel Tortillas	Super Lemon Mousse
7	Apple Cheese Wrap	Chimichurri Chicken and Pepper Kebabs	Brown Rice Stuffed Mini Beef Meatloaves	Roasted Turnips, Rutabaga, and Parsnips

Week 4	Breakfast	Lunch	Dinner	Snacks/ Desserts
1	Simple Pancake	Authentic Salisbury Steak	Beef Enchiladas	Pineapple and Mango Granita
2	Cucumber and Watercress Pita Pockets	Pork, Pineapple, and Peach Kebabs	Collard Stuffed Peppers	Vanilla Cookies
3	Bell Pepper Egg Muffins	Slow Cooked Apple Chicken	Roasted Peach Sandwich	Collard Chips
4	Apple Cheese Wrap	Herbed Haddock	Grilled Shrimp with Lime-Cucumber Salsa	Syrian Baba Ghanoush
5	Summer Omelet	Roasted Pork and Grapes	Beef and Rice Stuffed Peppers	Mint Carrot Rroast
6	Golden Blueberry Scones	Creamy Cider Chicken	Salmon and Asparagus Linguine	Tortilla Chips
7	Turmeric and Squash Omelet	Marinated Shrimp and Veggies with Penne	Brown Rice Stuffed Bell Peppers	Collard Salad Rolls

Appendix 2: Measurement Conversion Chart

VOLUME EQUIVALENTS(DRY)

US STANDARD	METRIC (APPROXIMATE)
1/8 teaspoon	0.5 mL
1/4 teaspoon	1 mL
1/2 teaspoon	2 mL
3/4 teaspoon	4 mL
1 teaspoon	5 mL
1 tablespoon	15 mL
1/4 cup	59 mL
1/2 cup	118 mL
3/4 cup	177 mL
1 cup	235 mL
2 cups	475 mL
3 cups	700 mL
4 cups	1 L

VOLUME EQUIVALENTS(LIQUID)

US STANDARD	US STANDARD (OUNCES)	METRIC (APPROXIMATE)
2 tablespoons	1 fl.oz.	30 mL
1/4 cup	2 fl.oz.	60 mL
1/2 cup	4 fl.oz.	120 mL
1 cup	8 fl.oz.	240 mL
1 1/2 cup	12 fl.oz.	355 mL
2 cups or 1 pint	16 fl.oz.	475 mL
4 cups or 1 quart	32 fl.oz.	1 L
1 gallon	128 fl.oz.	4 L

TEMPERATURES EQUIVALENTS

FAHRENHEIT(F)	CELSIUS(C) (APPROXIMATE)
225 °F	107 °C
250 °F	120 °C
275 °F	135 °C
300 °F	150 °C
325 °F	160 °C
350 °F	180 °C
375 °F	190 °C
400 °F	205 °C
425 °F	220 °C
450 °F	235 °C
475 °F	245 °C
500 °F	260 °C

WEIGHT EQUIVALENTS

US STANDARD	METRIC (APPROXIMATE)
1 ounce	28 g
2 ounces	57 g
5 ounces	142 g
10 ounces	284 g
15 ounces	425 g
16 ounces (1 pound)	455 g
1.5 pounds	680 g
2 pounds	907 g

Appendix 3: The Dirty Dozen and Clean Fifteen

The Environmental Working Group (EWG) is a nonprofit, nonpartisan organization dedicated to protecting human health and the environment Its mission is to empower people to live healthier lives in a healthier environment. This organization publishes an annual list of the twelve kinds of produce, in sequence, that have the highest amount of pesticide residue-the Dirty Dozen-as well as a list of the fifteen kinds ofproduce that have the least amount of pesticide residue-the Clean Fifteen.

THE DIRTY DOZEN

- The 2016 Dirty Dozen includes the following produce. These are considered among the year's most important produce to buy organic:

Strawberries	Spinach
Apples	Tomatoes
Nectarines	Bell peppers
Peaches	Cherry tomatoes
Celery	Cucumbers
Grapes	Kale/collard greens
Cherries	Hot peppers

- *The Dirty Dozen list contains two additional itemskale/collard greens and hot peppers-because they tend to contain trace levels of highly hazardous pesticides.*

THE CLEAN FIFTEEN

- The least critical to buy organically are the Clean Fifteen list. The following are on the 2016 list:

Avocados	Papayas
Corn	Kiw
Pineapples	Eggplant
Cabbage	Honeydew
Sweet peas	Grapefruit
Onions	Cantaloupe
Asparagus	Cauliflower
Mangos	

- *Some of the sweet corn sold in the United States are made from genetically engineered (GE) seedstock. Buy organic varieties of these crops to avoid GE produce.*

Appendix 4: Recipe Index

Printed in the USA
CPSIA information can be obtained
at www.ICGtesting.com
LVHW081148270823
756422LV00009B/666